IMPLEMENTING OKRS

JUUSO HÄMÄLÄINEN • HENRI SORA

IMPLEMENTING OKRS

The Practitioner's Guide for
Executives, Managers and Team Leaders

© 2023 Juuso Hämäläinen & Henri Sora

Design: Mikko Puranen
Layout: Eeva Lamminen

ISBN 978-952-94-7480-6 (softcover)
ISBN 978-952-94-7481-3 (EPUB)

Give feedback:
fast-track-execution.com

TABLE OF CONTENTS

PREFACE 8

ACKNOWLEDGMENTS 11

CONTENTS OF THIS BOOK 13

1 INTRODUCTION – HOW OKRS MAKE STRATEGY CONCRETE 14
1.1 How OKRs align the entire organization 15
1.2 How OKRs clarify what is important 16
1.3 How OKRs encourage continuous learning 16
1.4 How OKRs foster transparency and responsibility 17
1.5 How OKRs enable reaching results quicker 17
1.6 How OKRs enable the board and leadership to see
    the status of the strategy 19
1.7 How finding purpose in work motivates people 20
1.8 Summary and what's next 20

2 OKR THEORY 22
2.1 A short history of OKRs 23
2.2 Objectives 23

    2.2.1 The lifespan of an objective 24
    2.2.2 Only up to five objectives at a time 25
    2.2.3 Objectives are results-oriented, relevant, and transparent 26
    2.2.4 Objectives can aim at the moon or the roof 27
    2.2.5 Objectives are not subject to rewards or punishment 28
    2.2.6 Objectives are set at the team level 29
    2.2.7 Do not fear negative objectives 31
    2.2.8 Objectives are qualitative, not quantitative 32

2.3 Key results 32

    2.3.1 Key results are quarterly 33
    2.3.2 Only up to five key results per objective 34
    2.3.3 Key results can be stretch objectives 34
    2.3.4 The SMART key result 35
    2.3.5 Key results are not yes/no results 37
    2.3.6 Progress can be a key result 37
    2.3.7 How trust can be a key result 38
    2.3.8 Key results demonstrate progress 39

2.4 Tasks 41

    2.4.1 Tasks contribute to the key result 41
    2.4.2 Task, knockdown, initiative 42
    2.4.3 Objective, key result, or task? 43

2.5 Common OKR misconceptions 44

    2.5.1 "We have always based our objectives on the strategy" 46
    2.5.2 "We have used metrics before" 48

- 2.5.3 "Let's use this for project management or as a task list" 48
- 2.5.4 "OKRs will solve all of our problems" 49
- 2.6 OKR vs. KPI..50
  - 2.6.1 KPIs monitor how the ship is performing. OKRs pilot the ship 50
  - 2.6.2 KPIs monitor holistically, OKRs define the objective and end results 51
  - 2.6.3 KPIs and OKRs of a small SaaS 53
- 2.7 Summary and what's next 54

3 OKR PLANNING AND TRACKING 55

- 3.1 The cadence of planning and doing...55
  - 3.1.1 Planning vs. tactical cadence..56
  - 3.1.2 OKR timeline 56
  - 3.1.3 Vision – long-term strategic objectives..58
  - 3.1.4 Tactical – annual and quarterly OKRs 59
  - 3.1.5 Peace and concentration during quarterly OKRs 62
  - 3.1.6 Cadence of planning 63
  - 3.1.7 Same planning cadence throughout the organization 64
- 3.2 Long-term objectives are derived from the strategy....................................65
  - 3.2.1 Method: "What does done look like?" 66
  - 3.2.2 Method: "How might we?" 67
  - 3.2.3 Questions for converting the strategy into OKRs 70
  - 3.2.4. Using a professional facilitator 71
- 3.3. Planning short-term for a quarter 72
  - 3.3.1 Planning your first quarter 72
  - 3.3.2 The cadence of quarterly planning 75
- 3.4 Planning objectives in teams 77
  - 3.4.1 Handing teams the objectives..78
  - 3.4.2 Interpreting the objectives in the team 78
  - 3.4.3 Teams add objectives 80
  - 3.4.4 The model develops alongside the organization 80
- 3.5 OKR Tracking..81
  - 3.5.1 Tracking cadence in OKR...82
  - 3.5.2 What happens in the weekly meeting? 83
  - 3.5.3 The confidence score as an indicator of progress 83
  - 3.5.4 End-of-month activities 85
  - 3.5.5 Moving from one quarter to the next 85
  - 3.5.6 Retrospectives 87
- 3.6 Summary and what's next 88

4 OKR IMPLEMENTATION 90

- 4.1 Prerequisites and management commitment 91
  - 4.1.1 Prerequisites and What it takes 92
  - 4.1.2 Why is the OKR model implemented?..93
  - 4.1.3 Leadership commitment is essential 95
  - 4.1.4 Checklist of required skills 97
- 4.2 The implementation project..98
  - 4.2.1 Change management team..98
  - 4.2.2 The Internal champion - the OKR expert..100

4.2.3 The OKR journey – Futurice case study 103
4.3 OKR-software and systems 105
    4.3.1 Choosing your software 106
    4.3.2 OKRs on a whiteboard – case study Labrox 107
    4.3.3 Repurposing Jira– case study Ambientia 108
    4.3.4 TG software focuses on the strategy – case study Tangible Growth 109
    4.3.5 Reflection and engagement with KOAN – case study Aucor 111
4.4 Integrating Management Systems......................112
    4.4.1 Not everything needs to be ready at once 112
    4.4.2 What management system do we have?......................113
    4.4.3 OKRs highlight priorities 114
4.5 Summary and what's next 116

5 MANAGING CHANGE AND EXPECTATIONS 118
5.1 The objective is to improve business......................119
5.2 It's a long road from the initial enthusiasm to the finish line 121
5.3 Accepting that we are new to this 122
5.4 Objectives and key results are difficult in the beginning 124
5.5 Continuous improvement requires a culture of learning......................127
5.6 Radical transparency is the default 129
5.7 Change accelerates over time 131
5.8 Soon the teams will gain more autonomy 133
5.9 Summary and what's next 134

6 CROSSING THE VALLEY OF DEATH...................... 136
6.1 Confusion occurs when there is no direction 137
6.2 Lack of common understanding leads to sabotage 140
6.3 Anxiety is a result of a lack of skills 142
6.4 Resistance will grow if there are no rewards 146
6.5 Frustration as a result of a lack of resources 149
6.6 No plan means you are treading in place 153
6.7 Summary and what's next 156

7 WHAT HAPPENS AFTER THE INITIAL IMPLEMENTATION?...................... 158
7.1 Common cadences bring structure 159
7.2 The OKR model belongs in the annual clock......................160
7.3 OKRs will be used in all operations......................162
7.4 Rewards and OKRs 164
7.5 OKRs will impact your performance reviews 167
7.6 Towards an autonomous organization......................175
7.7 Financial Objectives Management and the OKR Model......................177
7.8 Changing OKRs in a crisis 178
7.9 Covid changes organizations' OKRs......................180

FINAL WORDS...................... 184
APPENDIX 1: TEMPLATES FOR THE OKR YEAR 185
APPENDIX 2: ARCHIVE OF CASE-STUDIES 197
SOURCES 204
WRITERS 207

PREFACE

This book, like many others, was born from the magical place between pain and excitement. Pain born from the fact that the vast majority of strategies and their related change projects fail. A problem that leaders around the world have tried to solve with various methods. Pain we have experienced when implementing strategy throughout our careers and within our own companies.

You can imagine the excitement when we finally found a working method after various methodological experiments: Objectives and Key Results.

OKR is a goal-setting framework that has transformed strategy implementation into something inspiring again. It has enabled us to improve the speed of change in our organizations, strengthen the culture of continuous learning, and increase the responsibility and motivation of our employees.

Driven by a passion for the OKR experience, Henri has implemented the OKR model in every company where he has been a board member. As an independent consultant, he has helped multiple companies in strategy development and OKR creation. He has also lectured on and given several speeches about the method. OKRs also play an important role in the work of Juuso, who helps customers with strategic agility and transformation initiatives. He's the founder of Tangible Growth, a company that combines novel leadership methodology and SaaS software to help customers ranging from Fortune 100 to startups. After Henri and Juuso advised customers with their early OKR struggles and helped with resets after failed implementations, the idea of writing a book seemed like the next thing to do.

Many books were already on the market, but we felt that one crucial angle was still uncovered by the existing ones: the how-to part. This book is the one to read right after all the inspiring stories about the superpowers of the OKR model, such as John Doerr's **Measure What Matters**. These stories can get you excited, but they also often leave you a bit confused. "What am I supposed to do now? What should I do in practice?" This book will give you straight answers to those questions.

First and foremost, this is a practical and straightforward guide that covers a lot of the change management and leadership required to implement the OKRs into an organization. The internet is packed with conflicting instructions on OKRs, and OKR software solutions are plentiful. Reading articles and following discussions are worthy endeavors, but what this book does is provide a clear roadmap so you can get these changes happening in practice. Getting started is, after all, the only way to start achieving results with OKRs.

Google has said it achieved time and again its objectives tenfold compared to what it would have achieved without the OKR model. A growing number of boards and management teams swear by OKRs because it allows for excellent strategic reaction speed, which improves strategy implementation. This makes OKRs the single most significant thing a leader can do to bridge the execution gap, i.e., to solve the age-long problem of how to make strategy a part of the daily work. Therefore, OKRs are becoming a mandatory part of every manager's education, and therefore we wrote this book.

The book was first published in Finnish in August 2020. Since then, a lot has happened. We've continued to work with the OKR model, lecture it to others, and help implement it with global and multicultural customers – and we've learned a lot along the way. Also, the book has gained popularity, and based on the feedback we've received, we managed to do what we set out to do. Create an impactful, concrete book that will help you in your OKR journey regardless of where you're at right now.

It was in our intention OKRs to do the English version sooner – but then life and one three-way merger negotiation, a billion-or-so dollar integration and other more minor things got in the way. Luckily OKRs adapt to changing circumstances, as you'll learn later in the book. You reading this English copy of the book right now is proof of that. We are thankful to those who have kept demanding it, thus making it an important goal for us. We're also excited because an adaptation of the book in French was published with Elie Casamitjana in February 2022, containing French cases like Peugeot and Société Générale.

You're holding a Finnish book in English, reflecting the Nordic way of leading and managing. The case stories are mainly from Finland, and they represent the lessons of Nordic leadership to the trendy OKRs. The good news is that the principles are the same worldwide. The bad news is that every implementation looks slightly different even within the same country. Often, the answer to OKR-related questions is "it depends"; this book aims to tell you what "it depends on". Hence you will need to adapt the model to your own organization, and you might even end up discarding some of the instructions. It is absolutely fine to break the rules, as long as you don't break the principles.

We'll introduce all the principles in this book but let us start with the most important one. OKRs aren't about the OKRs. If a company simply starts implementing OKRs for the sake of implementing OKRs, it will likely fail. Instead, there needs to be a clear intent, a business-related problem worth solving. OKRs are the tool for solving problems, but the tool itself will not solve anything. The people using the tool will.

This book is written for boards of directors, CEOs, leadership teams, change leaders, internal champions, and anyone considering OKRs or seeking support for an existing transformation process.

Start boldly. We have your back.

ACKNOWLEDGMENTS

The conception of this book began on a Friday night when Henri, a professional enthusiast, called Juuso. "I have an idea. We need to write a book in Finnish about OKRs." Juuso replied, equally enthusiastically, "Awesome. Definitely." After all of three seconds of reflection, the book project was started, once again, enthusiastically. One of the biggest contributors to the completion of this book project was that we, amidst all our enthusiasm, had the clarity of mind to ask Elisa Heikura to clarify our Finglish into understandable Finnish. Elisa managed to interpret the typed ramblings, Slack messages, and speeches of two enthusiastic men into succinct text with astonishing clarity. Elisa's understanding of the OKR model grew significantly during the project, allowing her to challenge our thinking in many places. Thanking you does not do justice to the work you did. Still - thank you, Elisa. You're amazing.

We would like to thank the following people for sparring with us and supporting our book. Katleena Kortesuo and Janne Jääskeläinen have significantly contributed to the book actively remaining on our minds. The working title of this book was The OKR Book. The name was inspired by a book that is practically a Finnish institution, The Strategy Book (Strategiakirja). Now, we have two go-to books: The Strategy Book and The OKR Book. Thanks to Tero Vuorinen for reading the book. I hope you'll see this pair of books mentioned together often.

It was no surprise to anyone in the writing team that the most perceptive comments about the book came from Jussi Haaja. Thank you, Jussi. The quickest comments came from a person true to his nature. Thank you, Janne Jääskeläinen. At the Chamber of Commerce, Taina Parviainen has acted with near-incomprehensible speed and precision regarding communication and manuscript versions. Thank you, Taina. You've made our job much easier.

A big thank you for comments, interviews and ideas go to Ia Adlercreutz, Margareta Fellman-Hämäläinen, Heidi Hyysalo, Hanna Kivelä, Eeva Lennon, Sini Kolehmainen, Mirell Põllumäe, Yacine Samb, Janne Ala-Äijälä, Joonatan Henriksson, Sami Hero, Timo Herttua, Jüri Kaljundi, Antti Kirjavainen, Julius Kuutti, Matti Lamminsalo, Timo Lappi, Ismo Salminen, Vesa Silfver, Richard

Snaith, Ari Tanninen, Teemu Tiilikainen, and Viljami Väisänen. We find it baffling how helpful people have been with their time to make this book happen. Thank you also, of course, to Elina Palovuori and Hilla von Essen for correcting the spelling of the book's drafts, for sparring, and for the encouragement. We don't think this chapter will survive your filter, but we can fix that in the blog posts you'll be able to explore soon. The English edition would not be possible without the help of Lwazi Vazhure, Elisa Heikura, and Mika Pehkonen. Thank you! And for everyone we forgot, thank you, too.

Henri would personally like to thank his family: Elina, Suvi, Seela, and Sulo. It appears that I managed to come up with another time-consuming project. Thank you for putting up with the project and encouraging me throughout the process. A word to my children: When school is over, learning needs to continue. The grades and the teachers will just be different. I think this book is one example of that. I would also like to thank all the people from Ambientia, Aucor, Labrox, and Uniogen. Our experiences are important to me. I would also like to thank all the companies, and the people, I have had the privilege work with as an OKR and strategy consultant.

Juuso wants to personally thank many people who have supported the journey and have made a significant contribution to his thinking, the book, general leadership, as well as life – There are too many to name, but here are a few anyway. You know who you are and why. Sheryl Wong, Lauri Siljamäki, Joona Joensuu, Jesse Niemelä, Andy Stark, Petri Viima, Jaakko Kankaanpää, Ingela Walhelm, Timo Vaajoensuu, Jari Still, Sameer Saigal, Lauri Asikainen, Jarkko Rantanen, F-Secure fellows over the years and the Tangible Growth gang. In addition to these people, I would like to thank the many managers and customers who have been with us on this path and dared to set out to implement OKRs in their organization.

CONTENTS OF THIS BOOK

This book consists of seven chapters. The first chapter covers the benefits of using OKRs. This chapter is intended for those currently on the fence regarding the usefulness of the OKR model. It's a good place to start if you need arguments to support your budding interest.

Chapters Two and Three go through the essentials of OKRs. Chapter Two describes in detail what OKRs are, and Chapter Three discusses how to plan and track them. Both chapters are very useful if you do not feel that you completely understand OKRs yet.

Chapters Four and Five focus on implementation. Chapter Four gives an overview of the implementation project and its steps, and Chapter Five approaches the implementation from the perspective of change management and communication. If you are already familiar with the OKR model and you have an implementation project ahead of you, you can start reading from Chapter Four.

Chapter Six focuses on the pitfalls, i.e., the issues where the implementation of the OKR model usually halts or crashes. So, if you have failed an experiment or your current situation looks challenging, this is a good place to start looking for the reasons why and how to rectify your situation.

The seventh chapter looks at the world after the implementation of the OKR model and tells you where the OKR model eventually extends its tentacles operationally. This chapter may be daunting, so you can leave it for now, and focus solely on gaining momentum. It is, however, good to understand how multidimensional an effective transformation is.

This book uses the terms OKR model and OKRs a lot. OKR stands for Objectives and Key Results. When the book talks about the OKR model, it refers to the theory, when referencing concrete items relating to a company, the book uses the term OKRs. Unless otherwise mentioned, the authors created the images in the book, a notable exception being an image used throughout the book, created, and graciously lent to us by Ari Tanninen.

1 INTRODUCTION
– HOW OKRS MAKE STRATEGY CONCRETE

The Objectives & Key Results (OKR) model manages the objectives of an organization. The story of the OKR model is the story of Google, as Google's success through this model led to it becoming more well known. In recent years, the use of the OKR model has become increasingly widespread and has been a talking point in many conference rooms around the world.

The OKR model is currently used by Atlassian, Slack, Facebook, Twitter, Netflix, Amazon, Deloitte, SAP, Microsoft, and Panasonic. In Finland, Motiva, Nixu, Futurice, tori.fi, Heltti, Talented, and Ambientia have used the model. The model is being piloted in quite a few other companies, but they're not quite ready to share their early results yet.

It's easy to conclude that more companies have at least tried to use the OKR model, if not succeeded with it. However, not everyone talks about their experiments. Very few succeed immediately, and failures are rarely publicized. Some OKR model deployments also just fail. The purpose of this book is to guide you away from the potholes on the road to success and also to help you navigate the more difficult challenges of change management.

Another reason for the lack of success stories regarding OKR is that many companies consider the provided benefits as a competitive advantage. When implemented successfully, the OKRmodel delivers on its promises of strategy implementation, organizational agility, continuous learning, and increased motivation. This chapter will examine the seven effects of OKRs that drive strategy implementation.

> **OKR COMPETITIVE ADVANTAGES**
>
> 1. Creates clarity and focus within the organization.
> 2. Aligns the organization.
> 3. Encourages continuous learning.
> 4. Increases transparency and responsibility.
> 5. Helps achieve results quicker.
> 6. Gives leadership an up-to-date overview of the situation.
> 7. Increases motivation in employees.

The OKR model improves organizational efficiency.

1.1 How OKRs align the entire organization

Leaders around the world are struggling with the same problem: turning their new, valiant corporate strategy into concrete action and visible results. Often, the objective setting is inconsistent, the objectives aren't tracked, and the objectives of different parts of the organization aren't aligned enough to ensure that the whole ship is moving in the same direction.

In the OKR model, setting objectives is transparent. All levels of your organization can see each other's objectives and align their objectives to support the overall strategy. The most important thing, however, is open discussion around target setting. Management objectives are derived directly from the strategy. They're being communicated to the entire organization. The teams will then create their own objectives based on company leadership objectives.

These discussions also lead to the fine-tuning and changing of management objectives. The wisdom essential to the objectives can often be sourced outside the board or the leadership team. When the entire organization is involved in the objective discussions, every bit of knowledge and know-how within the organization can be utilized.

A continuous discussion on strategy, the market situation, circumstances, and objectives ensure that the course of the company can be corrected at any time. This also allows easy detection if a part of the organization diverts from the strategy. OKRs allow things to be made visible and reacted to in a timely fashion.

1.2 How OKRs clarify what is important

It's not unusual for an organization to have a dozen change projects going on simultaneously. Excitement takes over, and tasks get started. And at the same rate, they are buried or left unfinished. This is an ineffective and frustrating experience, as finishing a project may be painful, but getting tasks done can be very psychologically motivating.

It can be difficult for a company to commit to implementing a new management model at a busy time. Still, it is in that very situation the OKR model is especially helpful. It focuses attention on what is important.

In line with the doctrines of lean philosophy, it has been found that the measure of efficiency is not the resource utilization rate but rather, the time to completion. Even if the whole organization is always overworked and busy, as long as projects aren't being completed, we can't call it efficient. More relevant than how many projects are in a pipeline, is how many of them come out of the pipeline completed.

The OKR model is a suitable tool to combat this. It reduces the amount of work in progress and shows where the entire organization is heading next. It helps employees prioritize their work and say no to sudden changes. Non-essential tasks are left for the future, and before that, objectives identified as important in this quarter will be completed.

OKRs also eliminate situations where key people are burdened with uncontrolled requests from everywhere. With the OKR model, only the agreed-upon objectives are important; the rest are put to the side and made to wait.

1.3 How OKRs encourage continuous learning

Although it may feel like an eternity when planning it, a fiscal quarter is a short time. The unexpected is always bound to happen once the quarter starts up and work begins.

The OKR model examines progress at a weekly, monthly, and quarterly level so that important data on relevant issues are tracked and visible. What prevents projects from being completed? What hinders achieving objectives? What skills are lacking? What resources are missing? What have we misjudged?

The retrospectives of previous OKR periods reveal many shortcomings in the organization and processes. The model does not point fingers at or evaluate the performance of individuals. Instead, it's geared towards continuously improving common practices and bringing to light any bad habits that have been adopted. The OKR model is a tool for development as a whole.

The OKR model also shows where everyone has to develop their work regarding self-leadership, growth, and learning. When work doesn't progress or slows down, the entire team is invited to discuss the actual problems and how they can be solved together. Furthermore, the ambition level set in OKRs allows people to set challenging objectives that they would not normally dare to.

1.4 How OKRs foster transparency and responsibility

The OKR model is based on transparency. All objectives are visible throughout the organization. Everyone has access to anyone else's objectives, allowing them to see the impact of their individual contribution on the work of the collective and the organization's overall objectives. Teams and individuals are more likely to align their activities to support the objectives of the surrounding teams and the organization as a whole in such an environment.

As both objectives and progress are public, the level of responsibility within the organization increases. Individuals, teams, and leaders cannot hide behind smoke and mirrors, only to explain why objectives have not progressed according to plan a year later.

It is important to stress that OKRs are not a tool for stalking and micro-managing people. Instead, OKRs regularly raise discussion about objectives and obstacles to progress so that it is possible to react promptly. You can ask why someone did not do something or what prevents the objective from progressing. The first question is inherently looking for a culprit and causes shame; the latter investigates root causes and motivates responsible action.

1.5 How OKRs enable reaching results quicker

The last and perhaps most relevant competitive edge of the OKR model is its speed. There are three factors involved in this. First, the OKR model can be used to respond in an agile manner, as progress is tracked every week. Secondly, things will be achieved more quickly by reducing the amount of work in progress and by effectively concentrating resources on what needs to be achieved right now. Thirdly, the OKR model uses stretch targets that encourage the organization to surpass itself.

Stretch targets may sound like they are meant to get more out of the workers, but that is not the case. Stretch objectives simply encourage individuals to reach higher than what the current level of knowledge would allow. It is more beneficial to pursue a tough objective and fail than to set a low objective and achieve it every time.

Tough targets motivate, great objectives inspire and results speak for themselves. Organizations that swear by the OKR model have found that individuals dare to try things they would not have otherwise when pursuing bigger objectives. However, this is impossible without a psychologically safe environment where failure is permitted. This is also not possible if the targets are tied to financial bonuses. Money is not the only factor motivating people to pursue great objectives.

CASE: The OKR model is important to Google for the speed of change

The birthplace of the OKR model, Google, is an over 20-year old organization of 120,000 people. Speed and agility are rarely considered the strengths of older large, global companies. However, Google has shown that it can constantly make rapid changes in any direction, with agile yet controlled objective changes.

Hanna Kivelä from Google tells us that the speed and dynamics that OKRs can achieve are very important. In the OKR model, the key is to think about balance: what are the longer-term objectives, what is being done right now, and how do we know that progress is being made? Every employee needs to know and understand what is important and how success is measured in the present, not in the next quarter.

With Google, the OKR process is done once a quarter. In practice, the company drives an organization-wide OKR process in a matter of weeks. For example, the objectives at the EMEA level (Europe, the Middle East, and Asia) are being driven through the country, team, and individual levels through all units very quickly, and it is a normal operating procedure.

Things are not left to be mulled, which in turn creates the desired and necessary velocity of change. For example, the transition from Mobile-first to AI and Machine Learning First was very fast, thanks to the

OKR model. As a result, in 2016, all product and engineering teams changed their focus in the span of only a few quarters.
In addition to the OKR model, Google does not have any other major management methodologies. Instead, employee performance is assessed separately from the OKR model in regular performance review meetings. Day-to-day activities are guided by KPI metrics and business objectives.]

1.6 How OKRs enable the board and leadership to see the status of the strategy

The Board of Directors needs to be aware of whether or not the strategy is being implemented. For this, the OKR model is quite an excellent tool. The OKR model allows management to know whether the strategy has been implemented throughout the organization by every team.

By looking at team objectives, it is very easy to quickly see whether the strategy has been understood and implemented on a practical level. As the targets are updated every week, the Board of Directors and management are constantly aware of how the implementation of the strategy's key objectives is progressing.

When the whole organization knows what's important right now, it focuses on what's relevant to the strategy. All change projects outside the strategy and the OKR model will either be outright rejected or at least discussed and justified before they can even be considered.

On the other hand, this also binds management. The direction cannot be changed at every meeting of the Management Team or when the CEO receives a new inspiring idea. Enthusiasm and ideas are vital, but they only come into their own when they are supported by systematic, long-term implementation. The quarterly implementation period of the OKR evens out the work and brings consistency.

This also helps employees stay motivated and focused. If objectives and current projects and priorities can change haphazardly on the fly, employees will not be motivated to make an effort to achieve them. Suppose an employee discovers that today's important work is not important at all tomorrow. In that case, they will naturally begin to wonder why it is worth making a great effort to achieve the objectives in the first place.

1.7 How finding purpose in work motivates people

The benefits of the OKR model are crystallized in the fact that the model is essentially related to the purpose of work. The purpose of work has become a topic of discussion in recent years, driven by **Simon Sinek**, **Daniel Pink**, **Patrick Lencioni**, and many others.

Simon Sinek emphasizes in his works *Infinity Game* and *Start With Why* how important it is for people to understand why work is being done. With the OKR model bringing transparency, and connecting strategy to everyday work, everyone understands how their work affects and helps others. This is important for motivation. In *Drive: The Surprising Truth About What Motivates Us*, Daniel Pink writes that purpose is one of three factors that motivates individuals.

The advantages of the OKR model are also reflected in Patrick Lencioni's books *The Three Signs of a Miserable Job* and *Five Dysfunctions of a Team*. The first teaches that we are unhappy in our work if we feel invisible and insignificant. With the OKR model, all teams become visible, and the relationship between their work and strategic objectives is made concrete. This is very important in today's work life.

The Five Dysfunctions of a Team, on the other hand, states that one of a team's malfunctions is lack of responsibility. For a team to take responsibility for what they do, it is a prerequisite that team members know what is expected of them. With the implementation of the OKR model, teams and individuals will be able to discuss their objectives regularly and how they relate to the organization's strategy.

1.8 Summary and what's next

In this chapter, we have examined the benefits of successfully implementing the OKR model. Many companies dream of an organization that successfully implements a strategy, learns from what it does, and simply achieves things. This is the biggest strength of the OKR model. Both the model and this book are designed for those who want to make a concrete change.

Concreteness is the key to the whole model. Instead of thinking and strategizing, OKRs are made available to everyone and tied to their everyday work. Things are discussed, tested, learned from, and based on what has been learned. They are changed. As this is now clear in theory, let's move on to more detail about the operation of the OKR model in practice.

2 OKR THEORY

At its simplest, the OKR model consists of two parts: the objective that tells you what you are moving towards, and key results tell you whether the journey is progressing as expected. However, the OKR model is not standardized, and there is no official rulebook for it. The internet is full of different implementations of the OKR model, and they all differ somewhat. This is both good and bad.

The variety of sources on the OKR model is bad because it can easily confuse a novice. The jungle of terminology and its nuances are like quicksand: the more you try to get a grip, the deeper you sink. Anyone interested in OKRs will soon wish that someone would come and unequivocally tell the truth.

Unfortunately, there is no single truth. This, in turn, makes diversity a good thing. Based on our experience, the implementation of the OKR model can go completely wrong when you try to push the model through force and without flexibility. Many people, especially in the beginning, miss clear rules and unambiguity as this would alleviate the sense of chaos and uncertainty. In practice, however, a great many things depend on the current company situation, which is good to be aware of.

For the OKR model to be implemented successfully, we feel two things are needed:

One, the initiator must have a sufficiently clear idea of what the OKR model is and how it works. We will present these rules of thumb and generalizations as if they were the only real truth to provide you with a sense of clarity and security.

Two, the initiator must have the courage to apply it to suit each organization – that is, to break the rules that we introduce in Chapter Two. That's why Chapters Three and Four talk about different versions and implementation phases. This chapter deals with issues that depend more on the company situation than anything else. Before moving on to the theory and implementation of the OKR model, a brief overview of the history of the Objectives and Key Results model is needed.

2.1 A short history of OKRs

OKRs are not a particularly new invention and are considered to have been created in the early 1950s. It was originally known as MBO (Management by Objectives), developed and popularized by Peter Drucker. Andy Grove, the third employee of the semiconductor manufacturer Intel in the 1970s, later the CEO of Intel, was also inspired by this model.

Grove introduced the MBO model and developed it further at Intel. Management by Objectives was converted to Objectives and Key Results, thus the birth of the OKR model. More information on Grove's time at Intel and the development of the OKR model can be found in Grove's book *High Output Management*.

In 1974, John Doerr joined Intel and, while there, learned how to use the OKR model. Doerr was later one of the first investors at Google and moved there early as an advisor. Doerr transferred his OKR expertise from Intel to Google, where its founders Larry Page and Sergey Brin implemented the model. Google estimates that the OKR model boosted Google's growth tenfold compared to what the company would otherwise have achieved. You can read more about this in Doerr's book *Measure What Matters*.

Since then, the OKR model has been implemented by many other successful Silicon Valley companies such as Twitter and Netflix. The model is gaining popularity worldwide, but its spread outside the IT sector has been slow, even though it is now clearly accelerating. In Finland, too, many have started adopting the OKR model and it has already gained a position in leadership culture alongside agile development and lean thinking.

2.2 Objectives

The objective is the most important concept in change management since without a proper one, change itself has no purpose. Each organization has various objectives at any given time. They are recorded in vision and mission documents and have been distilled into either a rough or very detailed strategy.

A company's strategic objectives are the basis for the OKR model's objectives. When a company knows which direction it aims to move in, OKR targets may be created from this goal. Since a company can only focus on a limited number of changes at a time, you need to decide what is most important to achieve first. You need to be aware of the first or next step on the path to achieving your organization's vision.

These objectives are meant to lead the way and be inspiring. An inspiring objective makes people take action and work towards a common future. It adds to the purpose of the work. Besides, it is good to be so clear and understandable that the language of the objective becomes part of the organization's language.

A good test for clear objectives is whether employees can easily remember them. They do not need to be learned by heart, but employees should be able to explain them in their own words. The second test is whether employees understand how their activities support or could support the chosen objective. Therefore, a good objective is inspiring and clearly explains what the organization is looking for next. Objectives may include:

- Our company is growing during the quarter but is more profitable than ever before.
- We're going to take over the American market.
- We're a great place to work.
- We are creating a whole new product for SMBs.
- Our customers love us.

2.2.1 The lifespan of an objective

The aim is to bring some kind of change, small or large, to the current situation. The life cycle of an objective depends on how long it takes to achieve that objective. At its shortest, the life cycle of the objective is one quarter, but in most cases, implementing a change requires more than one just one.

Objectives are usually set after the strategy has been defined and will change once they have been achieved, i.e., when the desired change has taken place. Of course, targets can also be changed if they are no longer relevant to the strategy. But unless it's a disaster, targets will be changed at the turn of the next quarter at the earliest so that the organization can rely on the permanence of its objectives.

Objectives will change as soon as they are achieved. Once the objective has been completed, the change it brings becomes part of everyday life and no longer requires any special attention.

For example, if you want to have a great workplace, it can include a wide range of activities. Moving to new premises requires a one-time effort. Similarly, tendering and switching occupational health care providers. On the other hand, handling staff initiatives requires creating and integrating a new process into normal operations. It may not be achieved in one quarter, and therefore, the same objective can – and often do – remain over several quarters.

2.2.2 Only up to five objectives at a time

According to the OKR model, you should only have up to five objectives at a time. Although it is acceptable to break other rules, it is generally not recommended to break this rule. One of the main problems with organizations is that there is too much work to do and too many projects in progress. When an organization doesn't focus on anything, it also doesn't complete anything.

The simultaneous management of several tasks, i.e., continuous contextual exchange and management overhead of multiple projects, creates significant waste. Multitasking slows things down, and work becomes chaotic and fragmented. If your own experience doesn't already confirm this, here is a diagram to provide a clearer picture of this situation:

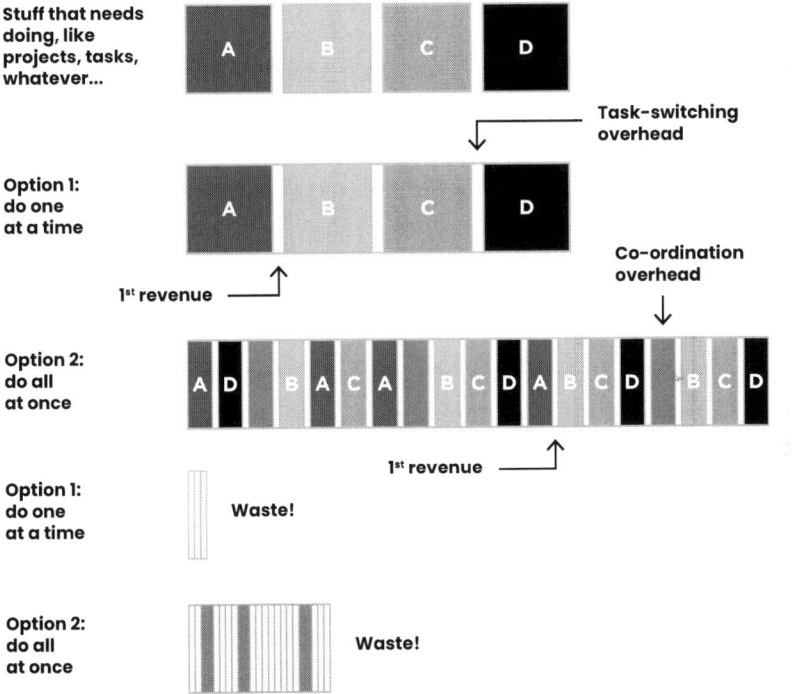

The cost of multiple projects.

Because, according to the OKR model, your organization can only have up to five objectives at a time, you must make choices. When the choices reduce the amount of work in progress, work gets completed. At the same time, limiting the amount of work also reduces the number of things to follow up on, reducing noise and increasing clarity.

You do not need to have five objectives. If it is possible to choose only two, you should choose only two. It is much better to note during the quarter that the objectives have already been achieved and new objectives are needed than, at the end of the quarter, to find out that everything is still unfinished and nothing has progressed.

OKR targets, as always with company change projects, are made in addition to the so-called standard work. Because work needs to be done, customers must be served, and invoices must be sent, you need to be an optimistic realist about how many changes can be done simultaneously.

2.2.3 Objectives are results-oriented, relevant, and transparent

Many management models and management cultures are focused on whether projects are on schedule or whether predefined tasks have been completed. It is still too common for the planning phase to precisely define what needs to be done, and then the organization starts to carry out tasks rigorously, reporting on its progress. The OKR model approaches it differently. The objectives are used to determine the outcome we want to achieve. OKRs give the organization the freedom to decide how to achieve the desired objective. The organization gets to decide the concrete steps to achieve the objective. Therefore, the objectives do not describe how to do things but what a good outcome looks like.

Traditional models:
- Are we on schedule?
- What's the status of the tasks?

OKR thinking:
- key result = get five new customers by the end of the second quarter
- key result = improve charging time by one second by the end of July

In addition to being results-oriented, the objectives must be related to people's work. An objective that teams cannot participate in or whose success they cannot influence is a useless objective. For this reason, each team sets objectives for themselves.

Management defines the top objectives, and then each level and team in your organization can explore how their actions affect the objectives. It's common for every team in an organization not to participate in achieving each objective. Many teams also have their own urgent objectives that are prioritized on a team level.

For a team to derive their own objectives from those of the organization, management objectives and the objectives of the rest of the organization must be public. OKR is a transparent management methodology based on the premise that all objectives and key results are public within the organization – every single one.

As a result, anyone can look at anyone else's objectives and determine what others are doing at any given time and what is important to them. This will enable them to align their objectives so that they support the objectives of their colleagues. Additionally, it allows for helping as well as challenging colleagues, both of which are prerequisites for growth and development.

Of course, laws must not be violated. For instance, if the publication of a particular objective violates the law on cooperation in companies or the regulation of insider information on the stock exchange, it cannot be carried out for the sake of legality. But once it has been revised and published, it will be an OKR objective, just like any other.

Finally, it is also good for management to make their objectives public in the OKR model. Management's work is often invisible and difficult to understand for the rest of the organization. OKRs make it possible for management to make their objectives visible to everyone. Employees who do not see what management's working hours are spent on, often find it easy to think that leadership is just golfing while the workers slave away. When objectives are visible to everyone, more trust is created inside your organization.

2.2.4 Objectives can aim at the moon or the roof

Some OKR objectives are stretch targets so that teams can boldly reach higher than they thought that they initially could. Stretch targets help teams achieve bigger things or objectives faster than usual.

There are many types of stretch objectives. Some objectives are feasible, although they require leaving a comfort zone. These are called roofshots. On the other hand, there are also ambitious objectives that may never be fully realized. These are called moonshots.

Google's mission is to "organize the world's information". This is an inspirational objective and involves a lot of stretch –so much that it may never come true. However, it effectively guides the organization's operations and encourages you to think bigger and more creatively.

The most famous moonshot is John F. Kennedy's "we choose to go to the Moon". It was ultimately achievable, although at first, it seemed almost impossible.

Moonshots distinguish the OKR model from previous objective management thinking, where the focus has been on achieving objectives accurately and at 100%. You can and must think much bigger in the OKR model. When a team aims for the moon, it begins to rethink its ways of working, questioning the common methodologies, and starts having difficult conversations that have previously been avoided. When the target is the moon, the team begins to wonder how far they can get. It's both powerful and empowering.

However, we must not discount roofshots, the more moderate stretch targets. Such objectives can be achieved during a few quarters and require only a limited amount of work. Yet roofshots can also cross comfort zone boundaries and inspire teams to surpass themselves.

2.2.5 Objectives are not subject to rewards or punishment

For the stretch objectives mentioned in the previous section to be put into practice, two principles must be realized:

1. If the objectives are not reached, there will be no punishment.
2. If the objectives are reached, there will be no financial rewards.

These are, in a way, the same principle because not receiving financial rewards is also a kind of punishment. Any punishment or potential economic disadvantage creates fear, and that threat causes people to set targets as low as possible. Moreover, individuals begin to partly optimize the completion of their own objectives at the expense of the well-being of the entire team or organization.

The fear of coming up short on objectives destroys stretch targets. No rational person is going to reach for the impossible if it can lead to something unpleasant. A large part of the problems associated with objectives culminates in fear of failure. Organizations commit bonuses, promotions, or assessments to the objectives, resulting in individuals starting a familiar budgeting game. Objectives will be negotiated as low as possible to ensure that they are exceeded. Individuals dare to experiment when their financial well-being is not tied to objectives. And when failure is permitted and, in a certain way, even encouraged, individuals dare to commit to the almost impossible. We will discuss remuneration in more detail in Section *7.4 Rewards and OKRs*.

2.2.6 Objectives are set at the team level

The rule of thumb is that OKRs are mainly set at a team level. There are a few exceptions to this, but let's go over the rule and the reasons for it first. Team objectives mean that each team reads the objectives set by management and creates relevant versions for their activities. In addition, the team can see the objectives of other teams related to their operations and align their own objectives with them.

A team has common objectives that all team members try to achieve together. Together, the team can produce much higher results than an individual could. Teams are always made up of individuals with different perspectives. A common objective allows everyone to contribute from their own point of view.

If everyone had personal objectives within the team, there is the possibility that individual team members would focus only on achieving their own objectives. There are also examples of individuals trying to sub-optimize their own objectives, even at the expense of team or organization-wide objectives. Patrick Lencioni talks about this phenomenon in his book The Five Dysfunctions of a Team.

When a team strives to achieve common objectives, its members seek to help each other. Together, you can change not only your own but also the team's methods. If one part of the objective is lagging, the rest of the team may scurry to support it. It is for this reason Spotify has publicly stated that they do not use personal OKRs.

There are exceptions. There may be a team in your organization that consists of only one person, although the word team usually refers to a group. In this case, one person can be responsible for achieving an objective. This is a perfectly acceptable scenario where you can set an individual objective rather than a team one.

Individuals may also have their own objectives. They can either be OKR-related objectives or, for example, personal learning objectives. It is, of course, important that these learning objectives align with the more organization-wide OKRs. Whether you should have individual objectives within a team is one of those things that is situational. However, the rule of thumb is that OKRs are set on a team level.

> **Case: OKRs for the entrepreneur**
>
> The editor-in-chief of this book is Elisa Heikura, who has her own one-person company, Elisa Heikura Oy (Ltd.). After listening to the writ-

ers' manifesto, she was convinced of the OKR model's usefulness and implemented OKRs in her own company.

A lone entrepreneur has to deal with everything alone, so allocating limited resources to the right things is crucial. But limiting activities is often painfully difficult because everything seems important. Each project has a direct impact on both the work and the results.

In the first workshop, the company worked out three objectives and 2-4 key results for each. Since the strategically important objectives of the relatively new company were to increase awareness, consolidate and grow the customer base and develop the products and services to be sold, the following were recognized as objectives and key results:

- The new content theme is processed into a sellable package
- 6 training sessions have been held on the theme
- 6 blog articles have been written on the topic
- There are 12 beta users in the online course
- EH Oy's (Ltd's) net sales grow to sustainable levels
- 12 new customer meetings
- 10 testimonials released
- 6 public appearances / content contributions
- 15 offers for over €1,000 sent
- The English version of the website is promoted from being the step-brother to an equal entity
- 100% of the English version translated
- The real-time translation process has been started

This meant that there were nine things to follow. To change the key results of the English-language site to numbers, they were broken down into operations that represented progress of 25%, 50%, and 75%. Google sheets were used as the OKR platform.

The objectives and key results were not refined with anyone else, which, according to Heikura, was not necessarily the best solution in hindsight, especially when two OKR experts would have been readily available.

In addition to OKR targets, the company is naturally responsible for both customer work and sales, as well as marketing and customer service tasks. The consistency in quality and the success of these are continuously tracked with a few KPI meters. KPI meters are described in *Section 2.6 OKRs versus KPIs*.

The observation of the first two quarters was that the three objectives were too much. When days consist of normal work, there is little or no time left for development tasks. The WIP limit, which is familiar from lean and Kanban, is in this case increasingly important.

In the third quarter, only one OKR objective was chosen for the company, which was to place a new online course on the market. The company aims to complete the objective in record time so that a new objective can be chosen even in the middle of the quarter.

After six months, the company has found that the OKR model also provides necessary permission for the sole entrepreneur to leave some projects waiting. Previously there's been extraordinary pressure to get everything started right away, whereas now the company is focusing on getting things done – one at a time. This has resulted in faster completion of projects and a decreased sense of urgency and stress. Heikura will continue to use the model in their company.

2.2.7 Do not fear negative objectives

Sometimes change is needed in an area that may seem negative or unpleasant. Management tends to both hide and dictate unpleasant changes. This may include situations where costs need to be cut or a product or service produced by an organization must be terminated.

In these situations, management takes over, makes decisions, and communicates to the organization that this is what we are doing now. However, the OKR model encourages a different approach. It is easier to accept an unpleasant or terrifying change when you can influence it yourself.

The organization also has a lot of expertise, ideas, and creativity to achieve objectives that seem negative. When management openly signals that an organization is under pressure to cut costs by 5%, it can be set as an OKR target. After that, each level of the organization and the team thinks about what can be done to achieve the objective. While one sees cuts to staff as an alternative, someone else may come up with limiting travel and focusing on remote meetings.

When a team finds ways to save costs, it becomes a common objective and not a hard limit dictated by management. It is no longer a lost advantage, but a means chosen together to keep the ship afloat. The OKR model encourages discussion and transparency even during hard times. Ultimately, however, the responsibility for difficult decisions always rests with management. If the cost-cutting target needs to be implemented quickly, management will take care of it. If it is a major strategic decision, such as leaving a specific geographical area or quitting a product, it is not an OKR objective. It's a managerial decision.

2.2.8 Objectives are qualitative, not quantitative

We have now learned the following about objectives:
- An objective should be inspiring, clear, and define the desired outcome.
- The lifecycle of an objective is one or more quarters.
- There can be no more than five objectives.
- Objectives are essential to the team's everyday work and are goal-oriented.
- Objectives should be transparent and public.
- Objectives contain a stretch element and can aim for "the Roof or the Moon".
- Objectives are not tied to compensation, and failure is not punished.
- Objectives are set mainly at a team level.
- A negative objective can still be a good objective.

Finally, we will go over the last principle of objectives, namely that the objectives are qualitative. In most cases, it is advised that specific, measurable, attainable, realistic, time-bound, and even big targets should be achievable numbers. However, in the OKR model, the instructions are clear: the objective is qualitative, not quantitative. The key result, in turn, is quantitative and SMART, as described in *Section 2.3.4. The SMART key result*.

An objective is inspiring and tells you what a good outcome looks like. It focuses on describing the objective and guides people in the right direction. The precise, quantitative expression of the objective is ensured by using key results. With key results, the objective is broken down into results that are tracked.

Normally, a good objective is always accompanied by an implementation schedule. For example, a business may decide that 'the American market will be conquered by the end of 2021'. In the OKR model, the schedule is not placed directly with the objective because it is an outcome of the implementation period. We will discuss implementation periods in *Chapter 3.1 The cadence of planning and doing*.

2.3 Key results

The key result is the second most important concept of the OKR model. While the objectives define the desired direction, key results are used to track the achievement of the goal through numbers. The key result is, therefore, concrete and numerical.

When determining the key result, you must consider what needs to be changed, realized, or completed to achieve the desired objective. Furthermore, the team decides how they will know that they have succeeded. Finally, a number to aim for is set for the key result.

The key result is not a meter, although it is numeric. A meter measures a specific situation. On the other hand, the key result measures the result of the changes. Once key results are achieved, they will have brought the objective closer to its realization.

Key results can also be inspirational, but even more importantly, key results are comprehensible. Since key results should guide the organization's day-to-day activities, everyone must understand the key results unequivocally.

For example, if the goal is "we are a great place to work", key results may include:
- The result of the employee satisfaction survey is at least 8.4.
- We have processed 20 ideas from the employees.
- 20% of the staff have enrolled in a fitness program.
- 100% of employee equipment allows for remote access.

2.3.1 Key results are quarterly

The OKR model can use time frames other than the quarterly implementation period, but the quarter is the one most commonly used. We, too, have seen it as a good length of time, because a month is often far too short to achieve significant results, and six months is too long. The world can change a lot in six months.

This makes the quarter an appropriate implementation period for key results that can be achieved in one period. Depending on how much of the key result is to be achieved, the key result can be considered as achieved once 70-100% of the objective has been achieved.

Not every key result for annual objectives needs to be set during the first implementation period. Only those that relate to what can be achieved during that quarter should be set. As the quarter changes, key results are checked, and new key results are created for the continuation of the objective.

2.3.2 Only up to five key results per objective

There is no reason to get overzealous with key results. No more than five key results should be selected for an objective. If a team has five objectives and each has five key results, it makes a total of twenty-five things to track. This is quite a lot when the team should also perform their day-to-day work.

We recommend that you implement key results in moderation, especially the first-time-around.

It is a good approach to set a few key results first, achieve them fully, maybe even too quickly during the quarter, and, based on the gained experience, increase the number of key results for the next implementation period.

Teams tend to want all the key results right at once. In this case, Chapter Five will serve as a guideline to keep the number of key results from becoming disastrous. It is usually easier to work a lot on a few things during the quarter than work a little on a lot. The more key results the team implements simultaneously, the more the team will have to divide their focus and the more things the team will have to keep track of during the implementation period. In addition, achieving a key result often requires that a wide range of issues and tasks is worked on. The more key results you have, the more things have to be processed and tasks need to be done. That's why fewer key results are better.

2.3.3 Key results can be stretch objectives

Key results can also be stretch targets. The key result of "we have implemented staff proposals" is very different if the target is five rather than 50 initiatives. Only experience can tell you what key results are easy and realistic and which are stretch results or absolutely impossible.

The terms aspirational and committed are used in connection with key results. An aspirational key result forces the team to stretch. It can even be a little aggressive and encourage the team to think differently and change their behavior. At the end of the quarter, 70-100% of the key result is usually achieved. The team strives to implement it fully, but 70% performance is usually considered a success, as the key result has been ambitious.

The polar opposite is the committed key result. It does not contain stretch elements. It is completely realistic, even mandatory. When the key result is agreed upon and committed to, the entire team commits to implementing it 100% by the end of the quarter.

For example, the release date, a big event, or a financial result are often committed key results. These are not flexible and require the team to prioritize these results. In addition to committed results, it is good to have stretch results so that the team can strive towards something more aspirational.

2.3.4 The SMART key result

The widely known SMART criteria works well when defining the key result. When SMART criteria are translated into OKR language, the key result is:
- **S**pecific, targeted at a precise area or object
- **M**easured, defined numerically, or otherwise quantified
- **A**ssigned to a specific person or team
- **R**ealistically optimistic, containing stretch, yet achievable
- **T**imely, possible to be completed during the implementation period

Take the key result of the review 'we have implemented 50 staff development proposals'. It is very specific if the staff development proposals are collected in a specific location, and everyone knows what and where they are. It is measured since the desired result is 50 proposals implemented. In addition, completion can only be defined as implemented when the person who submitted the proposal agrees that it is ready.

It is a good idea to define a responsible person or team for each key result. You do not have to record this in the key result description, but there usually is a field in the OKR software for this. If you are using Excel, you should create a separate field for persons in charge. We will explore available systems in *Section 4.3 OKR-software and systems*.

The key result of the 50 development proposals probably is a stretch result, unless only the easiest proposals are selected. If there are 1 500 development proposals in the queue, 50 may well be doable in three months. But if the development proposals need to be first collected, discussed, and then implemented, a quarter may be too short a period.

The implementation period should be long enough to achieve the key result. If it's a high-stretch key result, the team can be satisfied if more than 70 percent of the key result has been completed. In this case, 35 development proposals implemented would be a successful outcome.

Case: Aiming to improve the maturity of operations by using an information security index as a key result

Ambientia is an IT company founded in Hämeenlinna Finland, and present today in two countries and six locations. In 2019, the company had a strategic objective of improving the maturity of its operations. It may not sound very aspirational to an outsider, but maturity is very important in software development and inspires many programmers. This qualitative objective to improve maturity had to be translated into measurable key results.

One of the key results of the objective was: "each business unit has a security index of 8.0 or better". It implements the SMART criteria. The key result is specific, i.e. targets a specific area of activity, as the security index is defined precisely. Also, each business area is responsible for the security index for the services it provides.

The security index is tracked in an excel sheet that contains all known vulnerabilities for service offerings. The security officer updates the excel once a month based on the number of detected and reported security vulnerabilities in the systems. The person responsible for the key result is also clearly named. In the Tangible Growth software used by Ambientia, each key result is always assigned to one person. In this case, it was assigned to the business area manager.

The key result is realistically optimistic, as new vulnerabilities are detected monthly, and therefore, the team has to work hard and improve their processes to keep the index at a good level. However, the index can be achieved, and thus encourages teams to continuously consider security.

The implementation period for all Ambientia key results is one quarter. Within this period, this key result will be updated three times, so the changes in the situation can be tracked during the implementation period. Of course, the index can vary significantly from month to month because of the random nature of how vulnerabilities are detected in software. The key result requires continuous maintenance, so it could also be a Key Performance Indicator (KPI). The difference between OKR and KPIs are discussed in *Section 2.6. OKR versus KPI*.

Since Ambientia has always felt that information security is an important issue, the index is first and foremost an OKR objective. The objective is not easy, but it is also not impossible to achieve. To achieve the outcome, several scripts, or installers, for updating services were improved to make it easier to install updates. Similarly, testing policies were enhanced to improve the index.

2.3.5 Key results are not yes/no results

In determining the key performance indicator, the key result must not be a one-off result. It should not be possible to finish it in one session. If the key result can be achieved at once, it is too secondary or too modest. Additionally, the key result should not be a yes/no choice, i.e. a measure of whether something either occurs or does not. Instead, the key result should be a results-oriented number, i.e. the key result should reflect the desired outcome by utilizing a number that needs to be worked on over a longer period.

The achievement of the key result numbers should be tracked throughout the implementation period and should gradually increase alongside effort. It should require multiple tasks to be completed. For more information about the differences between a key result and a task, see Section 2.4.

There are exceptions, where the key result relevant to the objective may be in the form of yes/no. For example, "the office has moved to new premises" or "new occupational health care has been tendered". Theoretically, these can be assessed as a yes/no option. In practice, however, they are important results for the achievement of the objective and also require a lot of resources and time. They are, therefore, not individual tasks, but larger sets of tasks. In this case, the solution is to make the key result numerical by a completion percentage: "the move of the office has been carried out 100% ". We will discuss the percentage of progression within key results in more detail in the next section.

2.3.6 Progress can be a key result

Often, there are projects or other large entities that need to be completed to reach an objective. For example, "conquering the American market" can require many small projects that allow the overall objective to be achieved. Examples of entities include:
- Publish a US website
- updating product catalogs for the US market
- Opening a new office in America.

These are key results, but it's not easy to set a specific target number for the result. They can be converted to a numerical format so that the stages of progression are defined in advance as percentages. This way, the assessment of progress does not have to be carried out in the middle of the project based on estimates and feelings. If the objective is not clearly defined, it is difficult to say how much of the work has already been done in the middle of the project.

But when a rough plan for progress exists, it is easier to observe the situation objectively. For example, publishing a new language version of a website turns to a percentage of progress as follows:
- 20% – the contents have been collected and delivered to the translation vendor
- 50% – The language version is finalized and ready for content entry
- 70% – Content, metadata, and images are inserted
- 90% – The page is proofread and tested
- 100% – The site has been published.

It is essential for the key result that the granularity selected is significant for the objective's progress and that it is worth tracking its progress in the OKR targets. In this case, it's a good idea to use the percentage progression to track the key result.

2.3.7 How trust can be a key result

When it comes to developing the operational excellence of an organization there is sometimes a history of cross-departmental burdens, distrust, and friction. The situation can be remedied by raising the level of individual deliverables, which will improve trust and cooperation between departments. However, it is often useful for the director to know whether inter-departmental cooperation, communication, and trust are improving.

This is difficult to verify with a measurable quantity. However, you can work around this problem by using a trust score. A trust score is a subjective estimate of how much they rely on another department, team, or business unit.

A traditional trust issue lies between the sales and production teams. Sales feel that production does not deliver what sales have promised the customer in good faith and what is reasonable. On the other hand, Production feels that they would like to supply quality, but sales have sold services in a way that makes it impossible for production to function efficiently. This problem becomes transparent and measurable when you determine the trust both parties have in the actions of the other.

You can create any scale. Let's say the scale is 1-7, where the number 1 shows great distrust and 7 indicates strong confidence. Sales are now asked how much they rely on the ability of production to deliver. Similarly, the people of production tell us what their confidence in sales activities is. When the results are viewed, the causes and needs for change to rectify the situation can be identified.

The key result is a positive change in trust values. Regular milestones are used to determine whether there has been any progress. Changes in the index highlight the trust and atmosphere between the departments with enough precision to enable management to understand the situation and react when needed.

2.3.8 Key results demonstrate progress

In key results, as in the entire OKR model, it is essential to see the evolution of things. Progress – or lack thereof – is important information for planning the daily activities of both the individual and the team. Team leaders and leadership both benefit from this information, and it is also of interest to senior management and the board of directors. For this reason, key results are valued and graded, both at the end of the quarter and throughout the journey.

The planning and tracking of OKRs are discussed in Chapter 3. But for now, the most typical and simplest model will be given to demonstrate the progress of key indicators. The model comes from Google and can be called a traffic light model. The idea is that the progress of key results should be viewable at a glance, and for this purpose, the three-color traffic light model works well. Google uses a scale from 0.0 to 1.0 to value key results, and it is segmented as follows:

- 0.0 to 0.3 = red
- 0.4 to 0.6 = yellow
- 0.7 to 1.0 = green.

The accessibility of the three-color choices is not optimal, but it is used by most OKR systems. Thankfully the triad is familiar to everyone and is also intuitive.

Because the key result is numeric, everyone knows which number is the target and what level 1.0 performance means. Either the number is already in the wording of the key result (such as "We've implemented 50 staff development proposals"), or it's interpreted into percentages ("100% of the site has been published"). In this case, 50 job satisfaction surveys or 100% completed projects match 1.0 in the Google model. Key results can be stretch objectives, as even if the key result is only 0.7, it is still green, i.e., successful.

The progress of key results is regularly reviewed, and the key results are graded about once a week. By comparing the current grade to 1.0, the corresponding color for the key result is assigned. Colors show the overall picture of what's going on at a glance. Many companies that have implemented the OKR model have their own ways of scoring key results. It does not matter which type of grading you choose. The important thing is that it is understandable, is consistent in all uses, and that the figures are updated regularly.

Case: OKRs can also be graded "prematurely"

Often, in the OKR implementation period, key results are only valued when the quarter has ended. However, this is not the only way to go. A 20-year-old IT consulting house, Futurice, has implemented the OKR implementation period in a way where objectives and key results are graded just before the end of the quarter. This is done so that learning and preliminary results from the previous quarter can be taken into account when planning the next quarter's objectives.

This implementation period is justified when, like Futurice, you want to plan the objectives for the new quarter before the new quarter begins l. In this case, the grading of the current quarter is done a few weeks before the end of the quarter. This leaves about 1-2 weeks to plan the next objectives so that the following quarter can be tackled immediately.

The most typical question about planning has been: why do you have to do the grading before the final results are clear with 100% certainty? Knowing exactly what the final result is, is not the most important thing. It is more important to enable change in your own and the team's behaviors based on the lessons learned from the retrospectives. The objectives for the new quarter should reflect what you've learned in the past.

If tracking has been done systematically for two and a half months, the team should have a good idea of what will happen by the end of the time window. This and the confidence value of the team usually provide sufficiently accurate information to determine the focus of the next quarter.

Futurice has found that estimates given a few weeks before the end of the quarter are pretty accurate. Of course, not every grading is completely aligned, and some variance happens. However, the result is generally very close to the team's estimates. In addition, the frequent discussions on confidence values and progress of the targets during the quarter will guide teams to discuss and reflect on the situation.

2.4 Tasks

The key elements in the OKR model are the objectives and key results. In addition to these, it is necessary to break down objectives into smaller units - tasks. Task management is often one of the pain points of organizations and therefore, also impacts achieving key results.

Task Management contains a wide range of schools of thought and vast amounts of learning materials, such as the books *Getting Things Done*, *Deep Work*, and *Eat That Frog*. A wide range of methodologies is also available for the task management process itself.

How tasks are written and maintained depends entirely on your organization, the selected definition, and the system used. There are, however, six guidelines to help facilitate the completion of tasks:
- A task is a small, one-time thing.
- A task should be clearly written, carefully defined, and prioritized.
- Tasks should be recorded regularly and frequently updated.
- A list of tasks should be maintained for a week into the future and the following day should be checked at the end of the current day.
- The daily task list must not be too long, and the tasks' priority must be clear.
- It's a good idea to keep Friday's task list empty so that unfinished tasks from earlier on in the week can be completed.

The task is the smallest unit of work. The purpose of the tasks in the OKR model is to implement the selected key results

2.4.1 Tasks contribute to the key result

Sometimes individual tasks can be directly derived from the key result. For example, if the key result is "get 100 followers for a new blog", it can be used to generate a task to "write one blog article".

In most cases, however, one task derived from the key result has so many steps that it is good to split it into tasks. The subtasks for a blog article author might be:
- Think about the topic and accept it with marketing.
- Enter the first draft.
- Gather feedback from three colleagues.
- Make correction suggestions.
- Submit your blog article for marketing.

- Provide a personal presentation and a picture.
- Distribute the finished text on social media channels.

Section 2.3.6 *Progress can be a key result,* describes how a larger entity can be broken down into smaller pieces represented by percentages. This is often not enough, and they may have to be further split for to-do lists. For example, if the key result is "100 percent of the US language version of the site has been translated," the tasks may be related to different parts of the site or the steps related to the translation. For example:
- Collect the texts and deliver them to the translation agency.
- Populate the translations into the pages.
- Deliver the images for translation to the graphic designer.
- Make a ticket to IT for collecting UI terminology for translation.

A task can be anything that contributes to the key result. While the key result should not be a one-time performance, the task is. Task completion can be tracked by a yes/no question, i.e., whether the task has been completed. Plus, a task should be possible to complete in one session.

2.4.2 Task, knockdown, initiative

OKR systems, which are further discussed in Section 4.3 *OKR-software and systems,* often have a pre-built feature to record tasks in addition to objectives and key results. However, the naming of tasks is quite diverse. We have seen terms such as action, knockdown, initiative, and task used. In our opinion, the best term is 'task', which is one clear, small entity that must be done for the key result to proceed.

In addition to naming, each system vendor has its own way of dealing with the relationship between tasks and the objectives and key results. Because different vendors have each defined task in their own way, it often creates confusion — especially in differentiating between tasks and the key result.

The fact that organizations often have a task management system further complicates task management in OKRs. If a task management system is in use, you should continue to work on tasks there. There is no reason to transfer tasks to the OKR system. Tasks related to OKRs should be moved to the same system where the other tasks already are. However, if a task management system is not yet in use, most of the available OKR solutions are perfect for this purpose.

It is critical to the OKR model that in the internal language of the organization objectives, key results, and tasks are commonly understood. We recommend using the task as a secondary concept to key results to describe individual actions that promote key results.

2.4.3 Objective, key result, or task?

It is purely situational whether a particular issue is interpreted as an objective, a key result, or a task. The definition depends on, among other things, knowledge of the subject matter and the amount of effort required. Because the OKR model brings about change, any new change can be an objective.

Depending on the situation, a blog post can be an objective, a key result, or a task. If a single blog post has never been published before, the publication of the first blog post is a big leap forward, and thus this change is in itself an objective. If " publish our first blog post" is a quarterly objective, then key results will be compiled to support this objective and will be written as follows:
- Get comments from five people on the first text.
- Compare ten publishing systems.
- Publish the first text.

In this case, the tasks are:
- Email the text to five people.
- Create an excel for comparing publishing systems.
- Enter the text in the publishing system to wait for artwork.

Publishing a blog post can also be a key result. For example, if the goal is "promoting a new product to SMBs", then one key result is writing a blog post – or more – about that product. The tasks related to this key result are:
- Ask an expert to write a blog post about the product.
- Find the appropriate artwork for your blog post.
- Distribute your blog post on social media channels.

Naturally, a blog post can also be a single task. If the company's goal is to conquer the U.S. market, then one key result is to increase traffic to the US language version of the website by 100,000 visitors per month. The related task can then be to write a search-engine-optimized blog post for US visitors.

The objective, key result, and task are always related. They are determined by the size of the case, the size of the task, and its impact on the desired objective.

2.5 Common OKR misconceptions

OKRs have been around for decades, and the model is ultimately simple. It has been implemented in numerous organizations, and a wealth of stories about successes and failures have been gathered. Even those with success stories faced some stumbling blocks before the model was successfully implemented. It is worth considering why this is, in what is seemingly a simple matter.

OKRs are quite easy to misunderstand and confuse with other methods. One typical mistake is that OKRs are often thought of as a dashboard. Another typical pitfall is to get stuck in "we have had objectives before, nothing new here!" Another pitfall is using the OKR model for project management or as a common task list for the entire organization. The final pitfall is, of course, to think that the OKR model is a cure-all for your organization.

We will look at these pitfalls one by one. We have also dedicated an entire chapter to the differences between the OKR model and KPI meters. We have had numerous discussions on this theme during implementations of the OKR model. In the meantime, however, we will look at the example of how OKR models can be misunderstood.

CASE: "If you understand how the system works, let us know"

A software developer, who wanted to share their OKR experience without naming the organization they work for, or the customer whose project the OKR experience relates to was interviewed for the book. The customer in question is a large, multinational company based in Europe. The interviewee works in the development team, building an online store in a team of approximately 30 people.

Software developers operate as part of the customer's IT organization, from which business management has ordered an e-commerce implementation. The IT organization is divided into teams consisting of both in-house employees and external software consultants. These sub-teams, i.e., project teams, each build a part of the e-commerce implementation and report to the product owner, who in turn reports to business management.

The customer uses the OKR model, and when the interviewee started the project, OKRs became part of his work as well. However, the interviewee did not receive any orientation or guidance on the OKR model. This could be acceptable in a short, tightly templated project where implementation is related to a specific area. In this case, however, external consultants are part of a long-term development project that will be carried out over several years and is integrated into the organization's OKRs. In addition, development teams are expected to achieve OKR targets in addition to their work.

Based on the interview, the use of the OKR model has been confusing, to say the least. It is impossible to understand a big organization by interviewing a single person, but the developer's phrase "if you understand how the system works, let us know too," describes the situation quite well. The team has not had the opportunity to influence its OKRs; business management dictated them down to the team level. The teams have then had to adapt their work to the objectives. This had resulted in situations where a feature developed during one quarter has been unceremoniously dropped when the feature was no longer mentioned in the objectives of the next quarter.

OKRs are not the only guiding factor in the daily life of developers. Software development is also controlled by a separate release plan containing a more precise schedule and which market the new features will be published in. The actual daily activities are controlled by the Kanban board, which combines the features to be developed next from both the OKRs and the release plan – that is two different sources.

The progress of the OKRs are not tracked regularly, and the OKRs are handed down to the team quarterly. The team is then expected to act accordingly without guidance, further information or discussion. The interviewee says that the objectives that are already set on a team level can be found in an excel table, "if you know where to look for it." Reflections of the past quarter have been simplified to "let's try to improve next time".

The biggest source of frustration for the software developers has been when the product owner has suddenly put tasks on Kanban that seem irrelevant to the whole. The product owner has been pressured to do so from above, and these changes have been related to bonuses paid to one of the parties. The team is expected to implement the new requirement without any further questions.

This has resulted in developers feeling that the OKR management model is mostly amusing. It is not a work-driven and priority-communicating model but an additional add-on that creates more confusion and uncommunicated direction changes. In teams, many developers feel that the work would be more long-term oriented, clearer, and more consistent without the OKR model. When used incorrectly, the OKR model does not serve its purpose at all.

What can we learn from the case story?

You have to be able to see what is important from OKRs at a glance, at any time. A complex management model causes confusion. If the management model is complex and priorities come from many directions, people are confused.

OKRs need to be negotiated and adapted to the team. Of course, management can always force all objectives for teams if that is desired. But an essential feature of OKRs is to adapt them to the work of each team. Adapted OKRs will be in the team's language and build an understanding of the objective and commitment to the implementation.

Managing OKRs must be systematic and frequent. The OKRs are built around a systematic review of the objectives approximately every two weeks. This is how you know where things are going during the quarter, and this will help spotlight any problems.

OKRs have to be public. To be able to use them, OKRs need to be visible almost all of the time. Hiding objectives on a shared network drive doesn't help you lead.

People need to be trained in the OKR model – including external resources. The principles of the OKR model are simple. However, the common vocabulary, approach, and understanding of what is important do not just get magically transferred by jumping into a team and starting to code. A few hours of training is needed for each team member.]

2.5.1 "We have always based our objectives on the strategy"

Sometimes, a comprehensive set of arguments is needed to convince a colleague or manager about the benefits of implementing the OKR model. The following summarizes why the OKR model should be implemented, even if the organization is already defining objectives based on the strategy.

The strategy should determine the objectives of teams and individuals. This has been true for a long time. However, in the OKR model, teams play a much bigger role in setting their own objectives. Teams also have the right to define how objectives are achieved – unlike many old models where the objective may have been just progressing in a predefined project or completing preset tasks.

In addition, in the OKR model, teams take more responsibility for supporting other teams. Teams also take more responsibility for receiving necessary support from other teams. The OKR model aligns team objectives more effectively than legacy objective models, such as Must-Win Battles or the Balanced Scorecard. Although organizations may have created objectives and metrics before, most organizations do not track them frequently enough. It may be that the targets are revisited once a quarter, but at worst they are only reviewed once a year. This can happen especially if the objectives are hidden in the depths of HR software and teams aren't able to view and update the progress of the objectives themselves. In this case, the objectives do not actually steer the organization's operations. The OKR model provides ready-made tracking templates and implementation periods for this solution, which are discussed in more detail in the next chapter.

An organization usually has a lot of objectives, probably too many. In many organizations, the objectives are an inexhaustible pool of forward-looking fantasies that no one knows what to do with. In the OKR model, there are only a few objectives and only the selected objectives are focused on; the rest is not as important right now. Very few other models take as much of a stand on this as the OKR model.

The OKR model differs from other target models in that it encourages stretch. Teams set difficult objectives, enjoy the pursuit of great things and dare to fail. The OKR model is not only about objectives but also about the culture that supports them. In particular, it stresses the importance of safety.

The OKR model also takes a stand on management. Aligning objectives with regular discussions changes the organization's communication culture. Walking through OKRs is a part of all management mechanisms, including team meetings, one-on-one meetings, staff info sessions, and annual company reviews. All of these should be tied to the OKRs.

The OKR model also differs from the old objective management models with its radical transparency. All objectives, including management objectives, are visible to everyone and are easy to find and view. In this respect, the OKR model is different from old models, where some of the objectives are intentionally hidden. We have heard the phrase 'We have done objectives before, there is nothing new here'. However, we have never come across a situation where the organization in question would have had objective management on the same level as the OKR model. That's why you should familiarize yourself with the OKR model in greater depth before deciding that it has nothing new to give you.

2.5.2 "We have used metrics before"

The OKR model is often confused with other organization meters. OKRs are not a dashboard, although they have numeric key results. This confusion is understandable because often, results are *measured*.

The OKR model does not measure the performance of an organization. The OKR model is not a dashboard that can be used to check the current situation of your company. The daily business can be metered with KPI meters or scorecards.

Instead, the OKR model is a concrete model for managing change, and it shows how the desired changes are progressing. The role of the OKR model is to help the organization focus and push through changes that are relevant to the strategy.

Since this dichotomy is not quite self-evident and understanding it is essential for the implementation of the OKR model, we will go through the difference between the OKR model and the KPI meters in more detail in Section 2.6 OKR versus KPI.

2.5.3 "Let's use this for project management or as a task list"

Organizations are usually project-oriented, i.e., things are thought of like projects, and work is managed as projects. Therefore, it is not uncommon to try to use the OKR model and its software system as a project management system.

However, a project is only one way to achieve the desired objective. Although the key result may be to complete a project, the project is just an implementation method, not a purpose. It is not useful to view the OKR model and its system as a project management system. There are many systems better for project management, such as Basecamp, Monday, or Jira. The OKR model is used to manage objectives and results, not projects.

Another misstep is to try to make the OKR model a common to-do list for the whole company. It is true that tasks can be managed in an OKR system. However, it is not beneficial to manage all tasks using an OKR system – for example, customer support requests belong in a ticketing system, a sales pipeline in a CRM, etc.

This misstep is often the result of the OKR model's efforts to be the only source of priority lists for the staff. It is, however, meant to replace all scattered requirements and align the organization on a common objective. This may lead to the feeling that all other work should be displayed in the OKR system.

It is not the intention that OKRs are used to manage operational work, tickets, projects, budgeting, or sales contacts. Managing operational work is done in dedicated systems such as project, task, and CRM systems, or excel. The OKR system does, however, show the direction and the state of objectives.

2.5.4 "OKRs will solve all of our problems"

Like any other model, the OKR model is not the solution to all the problems in an organization. The OKR model can bring relief to many situations and also help fix many fundamental problems. There are still a few things that the OKR model cannot fix.

The OKR model does not correct bad strategic choices. If the strategy is already poor, the objectives and key results will still take the organization in an undesirable direction. In principle, the OKR model will show you whether the strategy is the right one in a few quarters. You will see if it is difficult to achieve key results in a few quarters and if objectives are reachable. If the results are not good, you should challenge the actual strategy – the OKR model is not to blame if bad choices have been made in terms of strategy.

The OKR model does not correct unruly behavior. If an organization does not know how to operate systematically, no management methodology can help. If weekly meetings are ignored, systems are not updated, and the explanation is always that "we were busy ", no management methodology can help. The OKR model can calm such a situation and can also be used to increase systematic work. Still, in that case, routine operations must be the first objective before starting on anything else.

The OKR model doesn't fix a lack of competence. If the organization does not have the right skills to implement the strategy, the management methodology will not do it magically. The results are not better than the sum of competence of the individuals who implement it. The OKR model can make the missing competency visible more quickly as teams discuss objectives and their own roles. Therefore, if the lack of competence of individuals is an obstacle to implementing the strategy, you should first consider how to assemble the right teams or how to increase the teams' competence. The OKR model does not correct poor HR management, such as micro-management. In the OKR model, you have to trust that people choose the objectives that are relevant to the organization and that the objectives are reachable. Of course, people may need help and support, but in principle, people should rely on their own ability to perform.

Finally, the OKR model both speeds up and slows down the organization. Depending on your organization, the quarterly status report may be either a fast or slow cycle compared to the previous model. For many large corporations, the OKR model brings considerable agility and speed. For startups, however, a quarter may seem like an eternity. The OKR model does not make time go faster or slower, but it changes the organization's perception of time.

These were the most typical misconceptions about the OKR model. But perhaps the single biggest question we have come across time and time again, is what is the difference between the OKR model and KPIs. Let's examine the difference between the two.

2.6 OKR vs. KPI

Key Performance Indicators (KPI) and OKRs have a lot in common. It is therefore necessary to understand the difference between OKRs and KPIs to ensure that the OKR model is deployed successfully. In OKR implementations we often encounter problems where the root causes and roles of the two have become blurred. OKR may encroach on KPIs, even when both are needed. The mixing of OKR and KPI meters is due to the difference being quite challenging to understand and not easy to explain. In this section, we do our best to clarify the matter, first through metaphor, then a little more theoretically and finally by example.

2.6.1 KPIs monitor how the ship is performing. OKRs pilot the ship

If you think of the organization as a ship then the roles of KPI meters and the OKR system can be described as follows: KPIs are the instrument cluster that tells us that everything in the engine room is healthy. The KPIs are monitoring that the ship pushes on as usual. KPI meters show that the boiler pressure is good, there is enough fuel left, the crew is at full strength and that there are a suitable number of people on board. In other words, the ship operates as it is intended.

If the KPI meters remain green and no significant changes happen there is no need to worry. It is only if there is a radical change in the results of the KPI meters that it is necessary to investigate where the fault is and correct it so that normal operations can resume.

OKRs are the ship's navigation system. If a ship travels on autopilot between two islands day in day out, year after year, it does not need an OKR system as KPIs are sufficient. But as soon as the ship needs a new direction or any changes are made, an OKR system becomes necessary.

The OKRs show the ship's course and speed. OKRs are also urgently needed if we are on a collision course with an iceberg. The OKR system controls the resources used to create, develop, change and pursue objectives.

The OKR model is not required if the ship's sole objective is to perform as it has been up to now. However, change happens in every company. Most want to grow, markets will create pressure to change, there is churn or change just happens organically over time. That's why you will find there are very few ships that don't need both KPI meters and OKRs.

2.6.2 KPIs monitor holistically, OKRs define the objective and end results

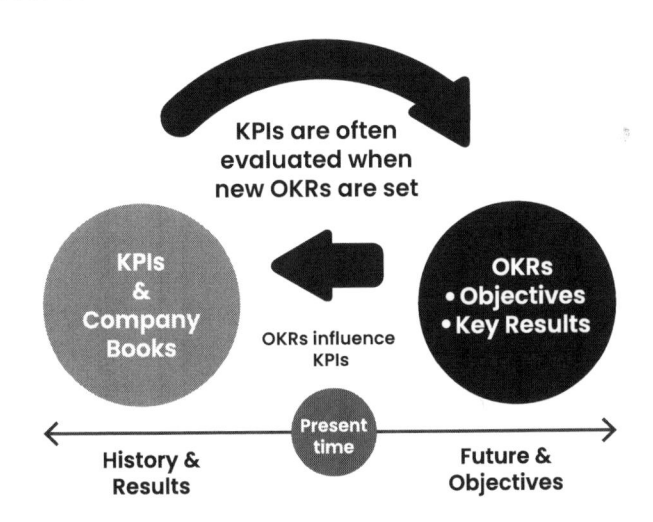

The difference between OKRs and KPIs

In short, KPIs are not the same as OKRs. The main difference is that KPIs are metrics, while OKRs are results-oriented key results. In general, there are many KPI meters in an organization, sometimes dozens. Each department has its own. They are used to track that everything works efficiently. Instead, a company has only a few OKRs which the entire organization works towards.

Although it is possible to use forward-looking KPIs; KPIs usually describe what has already happened. They show how the measures already taken have affected the whole, that is, what the situation looks like now. OKRs on the other hand are forward-looking objectives. They'll tell you where to go next. Part of the KPIs may be set as OKR targets. In particular, if one of the KPI gauges suddenly swings up or down, it may require a response with an OKR.

On the other hand, metrics that are at an acceptable level and are not critical to the desired change may not need any response during the OKR implementation period. OKRs focus on achieving change and new objectives. One of the desired changes is made the main objective, and all excess time and energy are directed towards its implementation. However, this does not mean that normal operations and, consequently, the KPI results should suffer as a result of implementing OKRs.

Change should be constructive and sustainable; permanently changing something in the organization's activities. It is not, according to OKRs, sensible to slave away unsustainably at a stretch target for three months to achieve an OKR. If this happens, the results achieved are likely to crash as soon as the objective is achieved and something replaces it as a priority.

Daily operations must continue normally, and the company must also be productive and profitable even in the midst of change. Sales tasks are handled, customers are served, services are produced, marketing is done, invoices are sent and wages are paid. Change-related tasks on the other hand change as the objectives are achieved and become part of standard operating procedure.

Implementation of the OKR model is intended to be a dialogue with employees. Since the change is carried out in addition to operational work, employees must be realistic about the day-to-day situation and optimistic in terms of objectives. If day-to-day life is chaotic and involves putting out fires, there is not a lot of time for a managed change. If you have an hour a week to develop something, you need to adjust the size of your objectives accordingly. On the other hand, if you want to make bigger changes, you should manage the workload of the employees. It is good to consider what can be reprioritized, or even abandoned, to bring about change.

KPIs and OKRs to support each other, together they track operational performance and strategic change. When both are in place, management has a clear picture of the company's activities, strengths and weaknesses.

2.6.3 KPIs and OKRs of a small SaaS

The KPIs show how the company is performing now, which helps you evaluate how the company is likely to perform in the future. For example, if you consider any small Software as a Service company, its KPI metrics include:
- Revenue
- Order renewals
- Profitability
- Funnel size
- Number of leads
- Customer satisfaction

If all the KPIs have been at a good level for a long time and the figures seem stable, there is no need to address them. When a company's operations are running smoothly, none of these need to be raised as an objective.

Imagine a situation where the SaaS company has found out that supplementary sales have recently been weak. For this reason, supplementary sales are chosen as the next objective, and the entire organization will focus on it for the next three months – or even a year if a permanent change is not achieved in three months. The supplemental sales will, therefore, become the company's OKR objective and the key results will be tied to the improvement of supplemental sales.

It is possible that during the first quarter, the pursuit of supplemental sales has caused a distraction elsewhere. As a result, supplemental sales have started to improve, but at the same time, for instance, customer satisfaction may have experienced a radical drop.

In this case, returning customer satisfaction to a normal level is raised as an OKR objective for the second quarter, alongside supplemental sales. This will keep the original supplemental sales target in place, but attention will also be paid to the sagging customer satisfaction KPI meter.

When at the beginning of the third quarter, customer satisfaction has returned to an appropriate KPI level, supplemental sales again becomes the sole focus.

After a year the OKR objective has been achieved and the supplemental sales are on a higher level. Supplemental sales are added to the KPI metrics and now its implementation is tracked like any other KPI. When it is time for the SaaS company to plan the OKRs for the following year, they can choose a new change as the objective. The KPI metrics are checked to ensure that the previous changes remain successful.

2.7 Summary and what's next

In this chapter, we have walked through the basic theory of the OKR model. After this, the reader should master the answers to the following questions:
- What are objectives and key results?
- What are tasks?
- How are the objective, key result, and task related?
- What is a stretch objective?
- How do I turn a project or a large entity into a key result?
- What is the difference between OKRs and KPIs?
- What are OKRs not?

In addition to these, we hope that it is clear that OKR is a management model based on openness and transparency. And that it will encourage you to make choices and focus on a small number of changes at a time. Before moving forward, it would also be good to understand what OKRs are not suitable for and what they do not fix.

Now that you understand the basic theory, we will progress to the actual use of the OKR model. The following section explains how to create OKRs, how to track them, and what a typical cadence of OKR implementation is. The section presents the different implementation periods and why they are needed. Also, we will start breaking the rules.

3 OKR PLANNING AND TRACKING

The strength of the OKR model is achieved through systematic and rigorous implementation. Objectives and key results alone, no matter how inspiring and stretch-worthy, are not enough. The effects are achieved by putting objectives into practice and into daily work. The planning and tracking inherent in the OKR model are key to this.

In the implementation of the OKR model, objectives and key results will replace various floating ideas and wish lists. OKRs will integrate into all management systems, planning mechanisms, performance reviews and meetings. To prevent the OKR model from being another task list tool, the OKR model needs to be strongly integrated into the organization's current practices. This chapter is about how OKRs are planned and tracked. We explain ways to implement OKR cycles and align your company's objectives. We will try to provide concrete tools for planning, although the tools must always be adapted to the company. Let's start with what the OKR model will look like when the OKRs have become part of operations.

3.1 The cadence of planning and doing

Planning, implementation and tracking in the OKR model have a clear, consistent and repetitive cadence. The cadence varies slightly according to the company's needs, size and operating model. When the OKR model is taken into use it is intended to become a natural part of the company's existing practices and routines.

Typically, organizations already have their own methods for yearly planning before implementing the OKR model. Each organization has developed its own ways of deciding what to do at the beginning of the year and what methods are used to achieve the objectives. Some organizations also have consistent ways of tracking annual targets on a quarterly or monthly basis. The OKR model will be a part of all these planning and tracking mechanisms.

Organizations often lack the planning of quarterly objectives and weekly progress tracking . These policies typically need to be created when you start using the OKR model. However, if the company already has quarterly planning and weekly tracking mechanisms, these should be integrated into the OKR implementation.

So, there is no separation between "OKR meetings" and "OKR planning". They are the same thing. The company strategy and its derivatives, annual operations planning, and quarterly planning will help guide these sessions. In addition, there is annual, quarterly, monthly and weekly tracking. First, let's look at the vocabulary a little closer, what a typical timeline looks like and how different periods relate to each other.

3.1.1 Planning vs. tactical cadence

In general, OKR literature refers to the quarterly periods or cycles, as planning periods. We believe that this is a very misleading term because planning is followed by implementation. We have wanted to emphasize the outcome-oriented and productive thinking inherent in the OKR model.

We are systematically talking about the implementation period rather than the planning period. This is a conscious choice because the focus is on getting things done – not only planning on how to get started.

We have tried to use the most unambiguous and consistent terminology possible in this book. The terminology mismatch regarding implementation periods may seem confusing at first. But each organization should decide for itself how it will use the periods and what terms to use. If there is already a well-established word for the implementation periods in your organization, there is no need to change it. The names of the periods are dependent on the timeline that the company follows.

3.1.2 OKR timeline

Next, we'll walk you through the most typical OKR model timeline. A large number of organizations manage their OKRs and key results with this cadence. We must, however, remember that there are many ways of structuring a year and none of them are right or wrong. ; there are just different models that suit different companies .

If your company has a different cadence you should take advantage of it - unless the cadence lacks a short implementation period. Adding the short implementation period to the timeline is crucial for successful implementation.

If your company does not yet have a consistent cadence of planning and tracking, you should first try this typical model. After deployment, the template can be edited based on experience and feedback.

OKR-MODEL TIMELINE

- Vision Period – strategic objectives
- Long Implemention Period – annual objectives
- Short Implemention Period – quarterly objectives
- Q1 grading and Q2 planning

A typical timeline consists of three parts: a vision period, a long implementation period and a short implementation period. These are usually established so that the vision period is about five years long, the long implementation period lasts one year and the short implementation period is a quarter. **Since this is the cadence in which a large number of companies operate, we use these terms for strategic objectives, annual objectives and quarterly objectives for the sake of clarity and simplicity.**

In this context, we have defined the other strategy concepts as follows:
- **Mission** = Why the company exists. What is it that we want to change in the world?
- **Vision** = What the company wants to be after a certain time.
- **Strategy** = A plan and choices made to implement the mission and to move the company towards the vision.
- **Implementation of the strategy** = A series of measures to implement the strategy. These measures are OKRs.

Long-term objectives, i.e. strategic objectives, are derived from the vision and strategy. The strategic objectives are used to derive the annual objectives. Key results are also typically generated for annual objectives. Defining the annual objectives is very important, as quarterly planning is based on the annual objectives. The quarterly OKR, i.e. quarterly objectives and key results, are derived from the annual objectives. The quarter, or short implementation period, is the period during which things are done concretely and the period in which key results are tracked, preferably weekly and at least bi-weekly.

3.1.3 Vision – long-term strategic objectives

We assume that every company has some kind of vision and a strategy derived from it. It is a prerequisite for all change management because, without clear guidelines change can be vague and possibly even reckless. The vision period is determined by the time span of the company's strategy and is quite often five years long.

The vision period can, however, also be much longer. The long vision period and ambitious strategic objectives have been referred to as a Big Hairy Audacious Goal (BHAG). Jim Collins introduces BHAG in his book *Built to Last*. A BHAG is a very ambitious goal aimed for up to 20 years away. BHAG targets have been used to lead companies to success over long periods of time.

Perdoo, an OKR system provider, in turn, uses the term ultimate OKR. Perdoo suggests that the ultimate OKR can be from 10-25 years away. For example, Google's "Organize World Information" is an example of an ultimate OKR. Such a mission does not change or will not be completed very quickly, allowing it to influence strategic objectives for decades.

The length of the vision period is not its most significant factor, but the strategic objectives derived from the vision are paramount in OKR planning. As we already said in the previous section, if the strategic objectives are wrong, change management will take the organization in the wrong direction. This is why the objectives of the vision period are carefully planned.

The objectives for the vision period are generated by describing the outcome towards which the organization is heading during the vision period and which the OKR model is used to achieve. Such objectives include:
- We'll get 500 customers.
- We are on Gartner's Magic Quadrant, known internationally by analysts.
- We have helped 10,000,000 people with our services.
- We are the market leader in our industry.
- In four years, we will triple the company size.

When it is clear to the company how long its vision period is and what is being pursued during that period, it can move on to annual planning and quarterly planning. The implementation periods break the ambitious objectives of the vision period into optimistically realistic pieces.

3.1.4 Tactical – annual and quarterly OKRs

The implementation period is the cornerstone of the OKR model. It is the period during which things are actually done. All objectives and key results are tied to the implementation period. Before the implementation period, there is a planning period that details what is to be achieved during each implementation period and states what is to be done and who will do it.

Two different lengths of implementation periods are needed, long and short; to ensure consistency in planning and implementation.

Long implementation period — annual targets

The vision period aims high and looks at the objectives that will be achieved years into the future. Deriving concrete steps directly from the vision is laborious, as the objectives can be so far away that it may seem completely unattainable at the time of planning. That is why a one-year segment of the vision period is worked into a one-year implementation period, i.e. a long implementation period that is aligned with the vision but does not reach quite as far.

Annual objectives are typically only made at the enterprise level or at the highest, a business unit level. Teams rarely set annual objectives even though the idea is not entirely disagreeable. In general however, long implementation period objectives are company-level objectives.

Annual objectives are derived from the strategy and are usually also assigned relevant key results. Managing and planning annual objectives are discussed in more detail in Section 3.2 *Long-term objectives are derived from the strategy*.

Short implementation period - quarterly objectives

The one-year implementation period is too long to guide daily operational activities. This is why we need a quick, short implementation period. Quarters are short enough to make things timely, concrete and expedient but not long enough to raise uncertainty about the progress.

Teams create their quarterly objectives and key results that guide their operational activities. These quarterly objectives are derived directly from annual enterprise-level objectives. Fulfilling the key results of the quarter will contribute to the annual objectives.

Of course, the short implementation period may be shorter than a quarter. OKR software manufacturer Weekdone has taken this to the extreme; its short period is only one week long. Weekdone's philosophy is based on the fact that each person always plans his week against OKRs and implements his plan during the week and reports it at the end of the week. Weekdone also has quarterly and annual objectives.

The length of the short and long implementation period is up to the organization. What is important is that the implementation periods help to plan the activities consistently, further the objectives of the vision, encourage action and keep the cadence of work steady.

CASE: Cybersecurity company Nixu uses tertiles instead of quarters

Nixu has arranged their annual OKR work around quadrimesters instead of quarters. These quadrimesters, or "tertiles", are sometimes lovingly referred to as turtles.

At Nixu, using three periods instead of four has a simple explanation. When the OKR model was first implemented, it was evident that the monthly or quarterly cycle would be too quick and cumbersome for an organization that was not yet used to creating and setting strategic targets using the OKR model. It would take too much time to learn to set objectives, compared to the time it takes to achieve them. The one-year or even six-month cycle, however, felt far too long. For an organization that grows quickly and operates in a rapidly developing market, operational activities require rapid changes.

When a quarter changes, there are usually a lot of activities related to running the company occurring at this time. The Nixu OKR cycle is aligned so that the planning of the tertiles is done at a slightly calmer time. For this reason, the first tertile begins in February.

The annual clock is now also aligned with the annual rhythm of the consulting business. The first tertile from February to May, is a busy period and therefore, strategic annual planning must be ready at the beginning of the year. The second tertile accounts for the quieter summer season, from June to September. If the OKR period does not change at the end of the second quarter, then the holiday season will not slow down the implementation of the strategy. Anyone returning from their holiday will still know that the previous objectives are valid until September. The last tertile is yet another busy period and September is the right time to plan the activities for the rest of the upcoming year.

Joonatan Henriksson, who works at Nixu, has written his thesis *Building a Strategy Implementation Framework for a Consultancy Company* about the company's OKR model. In his work, he visualizes Nixu's annual clock with the following graphic. The dates for annual planning, which take place mainly at the beginning of the year, are also included in the graphic.

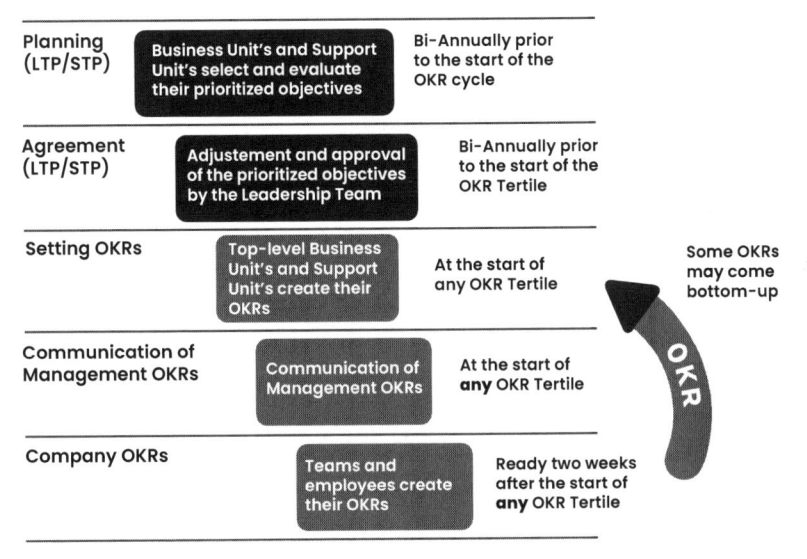

Phase	Action	Timing	Notes
Planning (LTP/STP)	Business Unit's and Support Unit's select and evaluate their prioritized objectives	Bi-Annually prior to the start of the OKR cycle	
Agreement (LTP/STP)	Adjustement and approval of the prioritized objectives by the Leadership Team	Bi-Annually prior to the start of the OKR Tertile	
Setting OKRs	Top-level Business Unit's and Support Unit's create their OKRs	At the start of any OKR Tertile	Some OKRs may come bottom-up
Communication of Management OKRs	Communication of Management OKRs	At the start of any OKR Tertile	
Company OKRs	Teams and employees create their OKRs	Ready two weeks after the start of any OKR Tertile	

Nixu's annual clock consists of tertiles (Henriksson, 2018).

Nixu's OKR cycle starts with the planning phase, which runs from the beginning of January to mid-January. During planning, business unit managers go through their top-level strategy and define the year's most important enterprise-level objectives. The planning also includes understanding inter-unit dependencies and prioritizing common objectives.

When the planning phase is completed, business units and managers will discuss the selected and prioritized strategic objectives together. This step is called the approval phase. The approval phase will be completed two weeks before the start of the annual cycle, at the beginning of February.

End of January
• Evaluation of OKRs

Beginning of February
• Fine-tuning of LTP/STPs
• Setting of OKRs

T3 October - January

T1 February - May

End of May
• Evaluation of OKRs

Beginning of October
• Fine-tuning of LTP/STPs
• Setting of OKRs

T2 June - September

End of September
• Evaluation of OKRs

Beginning of June
• Setting of OKRs

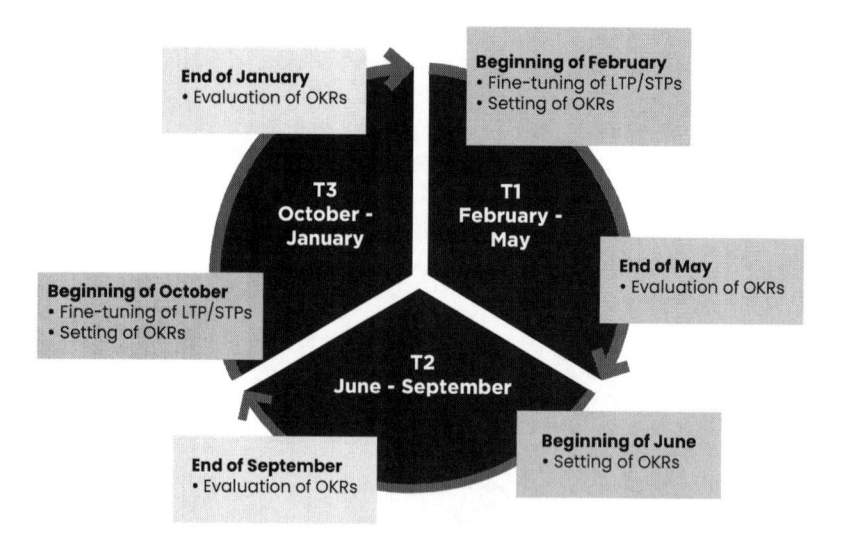

1 Tertile = 4 months

The Different phases of Nixu's OKR cycle (Henriksson, 2018).

After the approval phase and before the start of the annual cycle, it is time to set OKR targets for all units. Nixu calls this the 'Management OKR' phase. This creates tertile OKRs for business units, internal service units and management.

When the first tertile cycle begins in February, it starts with the communication phase, where the objectives and key results are communicated to the entire organization. Based on these, all teams and individuals create their own OKR within two weeks of the start of the tertile. This phase is called 'Company OKRs'.

Each tertile planning repeats the same steps starting from the Management OKR phase. Two weeks before the start of each tertile, the Management OKR phase is followed by the communication phase and Company OKRs. The planning and approval phases are only used with annual planning – or if there are significant changes in the enterprise-level strategy.

3.1.5 Peace and concentration during quarterly OKRs

The best aspect of the OKR model is the ability to focus on a limited amount of work for a limited amount of time. The OKR model forces you to select no more than five things that you consider important. These will then be the focus of the entire quarter. It is only at the end of the quarter that we will take a look at what will be done next and what has been learned from this quarter.

In the OKR model, objectives or key results are not removed or added without a very good reason. The OKR model also gives visibility to the cost of changing objectives. Removing one objective is not in itself a big effort, but if an objective is changed, the key results of all teams must be reconsidered and this can be expensive for the company. Therefore, objectives are not changed in the middle of the quarter arbitrarily.

There are organizations where reckless changes in priorities and objectives and the endless accumulation of unfinished projects cause significant stress and chaos for employees. The ability to concentrate on an objective for at least three months may seem utopian – but the results may surprise you. Teams can work in peace when management or customers are not constantly adjusting and prioritizing what is important and they can count on objectives not changing weekly. To do this, your organization needs to agree on two things:

1. What will be done about new ideas, observations, and other requests for change during the quarter?

Change ideas will inevitably come during the quarter, and therefore, ideas need to be stored. These ideas must be revisited when the planning phase of the next quarter begins. Ideas will bother and burden people until they're safely stored somewhere where they are guaranteed to be addressed at the right time.

2. If you are forced to change the quarterly objectives, how is it done?

Sometimes a change in the business environment can be very sudden. For example, a factory fire forcibly changes the quarterly priorities overnight. However, changes must be on the level of a fire, accident or stock market collapse; a very good new idea that emerged from a customer meeting is not enough. If a critical situation arises, you need to be able to make a change and chapter Seven explains in more detail how the OKR targets are changed in the event of a crisis in the middle of the quarter. The organization can also draw up its own rules and agreements for exceptional situations.

3.1.6 Cadence of planning

Now let's look at planning in the OKR model. What is the planning cadence, when the implementation cadence is yearly and quarterly? Each implementation period is preceded by a planning phase and the vision period is preceded by a strategy workshop or other similar planning event, where the strategic objectives are defined from the vision.

Depending on the organization, these are organized either every five years or according to another strategy cycle. The strategic objectives will also be renewed if the previous vision has proved to be poor or when the previous objectives have been realized. Furthermore, it is typical that strategic objectives are renewed whenever management changes.

Management plan the objectives for the long implementation period, i.e. the annual objectives, before the turn of the fiscal or calendar year. The progress of objectives and key results for the long implementation period is assessed at least quarterly, although management may follow up on these, for example, every month. Information on the progress of the objectives of the long implementation period plays an important part in planning the short implementation period.

The planning of the short implementation period begins before the end of the quarter. As a framework, quarterly planning takes into account the results and lessons learned from the past quarter, as well as the annual objectives. Changes in the market and the organization will also be examined. Quarterly objectives are tracked both monthly and weekly. Every week, teams meet to update key results and discuss the progress of the objectives. This will ensure responses are made in real-time and necessary changes are able to be made in the next planning session. With weekly tracking, focus is achieved as the objectives remain at the heart of the activities at all times.

3.1.7 Same planning cadence throughout the organization

Many have experienced a situation where their plan is at a stand-still because it has required the help of another person or team. Before being able to help others, teams first need clarity in their own plans. If the planning meeting of the other team is a month from now, there won't be any information on how quickly things can progress or whether they can progress at all.

This type of polyrhythm results in delays, creating frustration and lethargy. Waiting is one of the most typical and frustrating manifestations of organizational waste. Thankfully it is easy to fix.

The OKR model enables concurrent planning, which is hugely valuable and significantly increases the efficiency of the organization - nimble organizations succeed. To be successful with change, as many teams as possible must turn in the same direction at the same time.

Concurrent planning is therefore very important. When planning takes place simultaneously, feedback also flows efficiently in every direction of the organization. Understanding of the common focus is improved, potential challenges and team-to-team dependencies are detected in time.

It is accepted that in a large organization, planning and aligning objectives take a lot of time. They sometimes require so much time that waiting for every plan to be completed before the implementation period begins is impossible. Waiting for each team's feedback and plan to be completed would extend the planning and consume too much of the implementation period.

In these situations, management creates its objectives and aligns them with key stakeholders. The key stakeholders will then do the same with their stakeholders. Feedback is continuously collected. Even after implementation has started, adjustments can be made to plans based on feedback, if necessary.

In general, however, organizations can keep the planning cadence quite tight and concurrent. Each team always derives their objectives from higher-level objectives and also takes into account where possible, the objectives of teams they work together with. The less hierarchical organizations become, the fewer steps are needed when aligning the OKRs.

Next, we'll review methods of managing objectives and related questions. First, we look at objectives at a company level and how they are derived from the strategy. Then we will discuss planning team-specific quarterly objectives in more detail.

3.2 Long-term objectives are derived from the strategy

The OKR model is a tool for managing change and is designed to implement the company's strategy. It is, therefore, essential that the strategic objectives are known before planning. We assume that every company has a direction and goals which the OKR model will help them achieve.

It is also quite likely that the company will have some financial targets. The strategy, vision and financial objectives need not be fully defined to manage them. Some of the objectives or key results may be related to refining the plans.

Unfortunately, there is no single correct answer on how objectives are derived from the strategy. The best outcome will certainly come from involving people. Much wisdom can be found outside of conference rooms and in the operational parts of the organization, in customer interfaces, as well as in day-to-day work.

The strength of OKRs is that each organizational level is allowed to bring their own experience and expertise into the planning. Different levels of the organization may be present in the planning of strategic objectives, or feedback is received at the latest, when each level defines its short-term implementation objectives from the strategic, long-term implementation objectives.

Planning is usually done on one organizational level at a time and starts with senior management. Depending on the size and operations of the company, the definition of strategic objectives is done either in management. Management reviews the objectives and strategy of the vision period and organizes a carefully facilitated event for planning OKRs. The event will create the first draft of the annual objectives.

There are numerous methods to achieve this. We will present two methods that assist in defining the objectives of the long implementation period from the strategy. In addition, we are introducing ten questions to break down strategic objectives into concrete long and short implementation objectives.

3.2.1 Method: "What does done look like?"

The first common method is to visualize the end of the long implementation period, i.e., the end of the year. The key question is, "What needs to happen over the next year to achieve the strategic objective?" In the planning, participants will work on the following questions:
- What needs to be ready in a year's time?
- What should the implementation of the strategy look like at the end of the year?
- What will a good outcome look like in a year's time?

When the whole group has a mutually accepted, clear picture of the end result of the year, managing the organization towards this objective becomes possible. For management purposes, this outcome will be converted into objectives and key results according to the OKR model.

First, the common understanding of what a good outcome at the end of the year looks like will be turned into a verbal objective. Examples of verbal objectives are:
- Customer focus has increased throughout the organization.
- The sales funnel is overflowing.
- We are growing faster than the market.

These are inspiring and qualitative objectives in line with the OKR model. The key results are planned based on these and tracked to ensure that the objective is progressing as desired. The key result is quantitative and describes the results desired at the end of the year.

Key results may be, for example:
- an increased number of customer meetings,
- improving the percentage of customer conversions,
- an increase in the number of leads generated by marketing,
- improving SLA times.

When management completes the top-level objectives, people in the next level of the organization will interpret what they mean for their work. It is possible that in large organizations, business units or services will set their own long-term objectives. In general, however, the teams on the next level will only interpret the company-level long-term objective for the next short implementation period, i.e. the coming quarter. We will discuss quarterly planning in more detail in section 3.3.

Finally, the newer, more specific, or radical the chosen strategy is, the more time people need to find the right objectives. It is, therefore, very important that enough workshops are organized on the objective definition, so people can reflect on this. First-time companies need significantly more time than an organization that is already used to dealing with objectives and key results.

3.2.2 Method: "How might we?"

The second method we are looking at is an adaptation of the IDEO.org Community Design Kit. It is called "How Might We" (HMW). The method is usually used to design new services, but it is also great for deriving objectives from a strategy – with some adaptation.

The aim is to rethink the objectives in a way where the present does not limit the solutions. This method is especially useful when the strategic objectives contain a high stretch element, aim at a far-reaching future objective, or when the changes in the strategy affect the current activities significantly.

The idea is to forget the present and focus on what should change for the problem to be solvable and the goal achievable. The purpose of the HMW method is to reject all assumptions and existing structures for a moment and to think solely of the outcome of the strategy. For the method to work, participants must be allowed to forget the present and challenge the current structures and practices.

HMW workshops can be facilitated in many ways. One example is given below.

"How Might We" workshop example in practice

Firstly, those who participate in the workshop familiarize themselves with the strategy.

Secondly, the person who facilitates the planning describes the stretch objective and the time constraint as a "how might we" question.
- "How might we increase our turnover tenfold next year?"
- "How might we double the conversion rate of the current online store within three months?"
- "How might we reach all potential customers over the next year?"

The key is that the facilitator uses a suitably worded "How might we...?" question or "How might the world be different in order to achieve the goal?" The facilitator should also stress that it is ok to forget the existing solutions and procedures. And that existing structures do not need to be taken into account.

Thirdly, the brainstorming begins. This can be done by using post-it notes or other similar tools for collecting ideas. It is essential that existing processes, practices, or IT solutions do not limit the discovery of a revolutionary outcome during the brainstorming.

In the middle part of the workshop, each participant can present their ideas and views without being criticized. Depending on the participants, this may take quite a lot of time. Once the ideas are presented, the facilitator or the teams begin to group similar ideas. Here, too, criticism should be avoided. In the end, similar ideas are grouped so that they can be developed further.

When enough ideas have been generated, the best, most inspiring, and most functional are selected. Once the dust settles, the team explores what it just planned. It's time to compare the plan to the present. The next questions are:
- What needs to change?
- What can be changed?
- Who from the organization should be assigned to it to ensure the change?
- Who is the person who can authorize the necessary changes?

The team then writes objectives and key results for getting from the present situation to the desired situation.

The method is especially suitable for shaking up traditional thinking. Sometimes you can even do it too well. It may be that there is no straightforward way to move to practical steps from the desired end result. Sometimes the gap between the present and the future state is too great. If this happens, it is advisable to continue by using one of the other methods described in this chapter, to put things into practice.

Case: "How Might We" or HMW is Timo Herttua's favorite

Timo Herttua, who works as a Product Director at Hoxhunt, has noticed that people involved in the business usually have to think about things with constraints in mind. There are budgetary, timetable, technological, geographical, or restrictions set by an existing product that hinders imaginative solutions. The question "How Might We" is meant to get a reprieve from all this.

Almost all business development is a continuous improvement of the current state. For a company to get out of continuous improvement for a while, it needs the HMW method. For instance, backpacks have been used for millennia to carry goods and heels have existed ever since Roman carts. Outdoor equipment companies continue to improve the thousand-year-old concept of the backpack every year by making new versions of it – and still doing good business with it.

The combination of the wheel and the suitcase didn't happen until the 1970s. Amazingly, during thousands of years, no one came up with this combination of components, yet pulling along a suitcase on wheels is perfectly commonplace at airports today. Continuous improvement can become a revolutionary idea, for example by using the HMW method.

However, Herttua points out that it is not necessarily wise to combine the invention of revolutionary ideas with the deployment phase of the OKR model. Based on his findings, the HMW method is better suited to a company that already has experience in designing and challenging the strategy using various design thinking methods.

In the first strategy workshop after implementing the OKR model, other methods will work better. Once the organization is more experienced with OKRs, this model will work really well for planning stretch objectives and finding exceptional ideas.

When first using this method, you should be prepared for the fact that exceptional proposals will most likely not come during the first workshop. During the lunch break, for example, the workshop facilitator and the person in charge of the business should take a moment to plan.

In the middle of the workshop, the ideas that emerged in the workshop should be reviewed. If the quality of the plans is not good enough, should a few new ones be inserted? If they do not contain enough stretch, should the strategy be explained again? After all, the idea of the method is to escape the limitations of everyday life, even for just a moment.]

3.2.3 Questions for converting the strategy into OKRs

Traditionally, the strategy describes the change targets of figures, markets, and conduct of the overall business. Once the strategy is established in the organization, it is reasonably easy to squeeze out different objectives and key results from it. The following ten questions will help in breaking down the vision objectives into long-term objectives and the long-term implementation objectives into short implementation period objectives:

1. What is the goal at the end of the period?

If the goal is not clear, a good first-quarter goal can be used to describe it more accurately. Getting started pays off. You can't hide behind a design table.

2. Is there already a meter for the end result?

Does your organization's current dashboard describe the organization's situation so that when the meters change in the right direction, you also reach the desired goal? If this is not the case, you can list objectives for the development of the instrument cluster. If, on the other hand, the instrument cluster describes the situation well, improvement in the measurements will be the right key result.

3. Do we know what we don't know?

Often there are things in the strategy that need clarification. If that is the case, clarifying them are good objectives.

4. What could be completely unexpected?

Do we now recognize anything based on the strategy that could happen completely unexpectedly? How do you get ready for them? Could preparing for these be an objective?

5. What do our stakeholders expect from us?

What do our stakeholders, as described in the strategy, expect from us?

6. Is the strategy inspiring?

Is the strategy so inspiring that people in your organization are willingly joining the journey? If not, how do we inspire people more?

7. Does the organization's mindset or culture support the change?

If not, what do we have to do to make the change possible? How will this be handled throughout the change process? What skills do we need more of, and how do we get them?

8. What do we not want to do on the journey?

The OKR model does not normally focus on things that we do not want to do, only on things that will be done. What we do not want is defined in the strategy. However, when things appear during the planning that we identify that we do not want to do, they should be recorded.

9. What would be nice or interesting to do, but is not critical at the moment?

If these things surface, they end up on the "not to do" list.

10. How do we summarize the collected items to a maximum of five objectives and key results?

After a long time spent on collecting objectives, there are a lot of ideas going on. Eventually, a maximum of five objectives and key results need to be selected. Remember, a smaller number of objectives is better than a large number. Pruning ideas can be really difficult, but rewarding.

3.2.4. Using a professional facilitator

When the objectives and key results are derived from the strategy, we recommend that you use a professional facilitator, or at least a non-team member. The facilitator's task is to get people working, moderate conversation, arrange timetables, and document everything so that the participants can focus on the ideas and be productive.

Although a facilitator does not traditionally comment on the content itself, our experience says that in OKR workshops, the facilitator is often needed to interpret the objectives and key results. A facilitator with sufficient business experience, and well-versed in the OKR model, is a valuable addition to OKR workshops. A facilitator with knowledge of the OKR model is better able to help the organization towards objectives and key results that will accelerate the deployment of the OKR model.

The need for a professional, external facilitator is greatest in the first quarter and when the model is implemented. Over time, the team itself will need to get used to deriving and planning OKRs from the strategy. The role and expertise of the team leader as the leader of OKR workshops will become more important as time goes by.

A company accustomed to the OKR model can use any skilled internal or external facilitator for the workshops. However, it is always useful for the facilitator to understand the OKR model.

3.3. Planning short-term for a quarter

In most cases, the OKR model has a short implementation period of one quarter. A year is too long to wait for information on objectives and key results, too slow to achieve objectives in general, and too distant to plan your daily activities. As Marcus Buckingham and Ashley Goodall state in their book *Nine Lies About Work*, the plan expires as soon as it is done.

A quarter is an appropriate amount of time for a short implementation cycle. Objectives and key results are planned for the next three months, with a deadline of three months for reaching the key results. The lifecycle of an objective can span several quarters if it is not possible to implement it within three months. New key results are defined for the following quarters for the objectives that have not yet been completed.

When the quarter changes, new targets will be defined for completed objectives, if needed. At the same time, it needs to be determined if the objectives are still in line with the main objectives of the strategy and the agreed annual objectives, or whether something has substantially changed.

This section describes planning the first quarter of the year or financial year and the cadence of planning following quarters and aligning objectives.

3.3.1 Planning your first quarter

The planning of the first quarter of the year or financial year is preceded by management setting the annual objectives for the entire company, as described in the previous section. After this, the planning of the first quarter begins. If management sets quarterly objectives and key results for itself or the company in addition to its annual objectives, they may be completed first. However, it is quite typical that all teams start planning the first quarter at the same time, as soon as the annual objectives are completed.

The same methods as in the previous chapter can be used to manage quarterly objectives. The list of ten questions, in particular, will help when you think about what needs to be done first to achieve the objectives of the year.

Quarterly planning will decide which five objectives will need to be focused on during the next three months in order to achieve the objectives for the year. The quarterly objectives are strongly in line with the annual objectives. They aren't, however entirely identical, because when the annual objective is broken down into quarterly objectives, it makes sense to focus on the period at hand. For example, if the annual objective is "we have helped 2,000,000 people with our services", the quarterly objective may be either, "we have helped 500,000 people with our services", or "we have developed a new service". Both further the annual goal, but in a different way.

The quarterly objective will then be turned into key results, the realization of which will take the objective forward or even implement it altogether. The wording of the objective is an essential element in assigning a key result. If management first makes its quarterly objectives and the related key results, these top-level key results must be end-goal-oriented. They should not limit the scope of practical implementation of things when other teams interpret the key result.

Once management has completed the top-level objectives, people at the next level of the organization will interpret what these objectives mean for their work during the following quarter. This way, you proceed one level of the organization at a time until each team and individual has been allowed to determine their contribution to the overall implementation.

When designing the objectives and key results of the OKR model for the first time, it is good to consider the following:

- The first planning sessions require significantly more time than the following ones. In the first workshops, it is worthwhile to set aside a time for reflection, questions and hesitation.Organize several iterations so the end result can be fully thought through.
- It's much more important to initially complete some OKR-model objectives and key results and start testing them, rather than trying to get it perfect from the start. Learning is done by experimenting and repairing, not by theorizing and over-analyzing.

- Teams must be given sufficient support to derive their own objectives. The stricter the objectives have been dictated from above before OKRs, the more hesitant teams will be to take ownership of their objectives. This should not be punished or blamed on the teams, teams should be given more support and encouragement on their road to autonomy.

The team organizes a workshop where it looks at the objectives and key results defined by management and interprets how they affect the team's work. When you only have three months, it's a good idea to think carefully about what the team should focus on so that the work supports the company objectives. What key results show that the team has completed its part in the company objective?

The workshop can, and often does, involve a person from the higher-level OKR planning who can answer questions related to management objectives and key results. However, this is not necessary. The OKR model encourages you to ask and discuss management objectives when they are presented to the entire organization. Since all objectives and key results are transparently accessible to everyone at all times, concerns can be voiced as they come up.

Case: Google reWork guidelines

Google's own reWork guidance outlines the following timeline for the first quarter of OKR design:

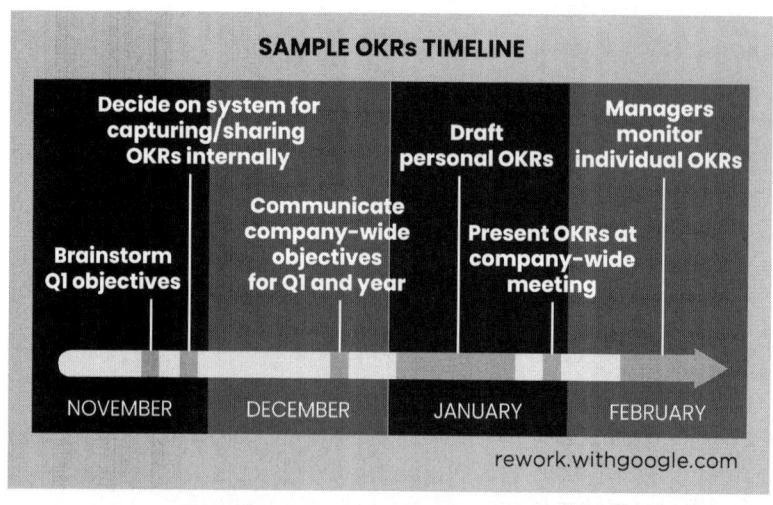

SAMPLE OKRs TIMELINE

- Brainstorm Q1 objectives — NOVEMBER
- Decide on system for capturing/sharing OKRs internally
- Communicate company-wide objectives for Q1 and year — DECEMBER
- Draft personal OKRs
- Present OKRs at company-wide meeting — JANUARY
- Managers monitor individual OKRs — FEBRUARY

rework.withgoogle.com

An example of an OKR timeline (adapted from Google, 2018).

In Google's model, the annual objective planning begins in mid-November. Management will communicate the annual objectives and its first-quarter objectives at the end of December. Teams have the month of January to set up their objectives to be communicated at the end of January in a company-wide meeting. From February onwards, tracking happens according to the standard process.]

3.3.2 The cadence of quarterly planning

Planning the first quarter of the OKR model is always a unique effort. In the future planning, implementation and tracking will be easier and happen according to a calendar. The cadence depends on the company and its needs. There are two options for designing quarterly objectives.

Interlaced quarterly planning

The planning of a new quarter often occurs with a small overlap with the ongoing quarter. Especially in large organizations, planning the next implementation period is started earlier, as it takes time to align the objectives.

For planning purposes, data and results relating to the current quarter are collected. Planning will also use recorded data on necessary changes, observations and other wishes during the previous implementation period. In addition, the strategy and objectives for the year will be examined.

Management plans its quarterly objectives up to a month before the quarter changes. This gives management enough time to communicate their objectives and gives teams enough time to have their own planning meetings before the new cycle begins.

Case: Ambientia invests in aligning its objectives

Ambientia starts planning the next quarter about a month before the end of the ongoing quarter. Planning starts with a senior management meeting, then a meeting with the management team to discuss and negotiate ideas. When the management team is ready, its members will have discussions with their own teams. This process takes about a calendar month.

At the very beginning of the quarter, an alignment day is organized within the management team, who will confirm that all teams have planned their objectives. The event ensures that the objectives created by the teams are in alignment with the company strategy. After that, the implementation of the objectives in the quarter can begin.

Whilst the Ambientia process is heavy, in an organization of 200 people it is still able to be implemented. The implementation of the OKR model aims to bring alignment to the whole company, so special attention has been paid to alignment.

The planning of objectives and key results has been implemented directly into their software system so everything is always visible to the organization which allows teams to monitor the planning of other teams. In this way, they can also think of alignment between teams when planning objectives.]

Consecutive quarterly planning

Some organizations prefer for the previous quarter to finish and for that quarter's results to be available before they plan the next one. This is possible, but planning requires very strict discipline from the organization.

- The results of the quarter need to be reported very quickly at the end of the implementation period.
- Planning needs sufficient resources allocated to run the plan through the entire organization in a week or two.

In this scenario, management plans their objectives as soon as the quarter is finished, and the other teams will do theirs in the first few weeks. The more agile and self-directed the organization is, the more likely it is that this model will work.

Case: Talented provides themes, teams decide objectives

Talented Ltd, which focuses on IT recruitment and growth consulting, recently implemented the OKR model. In three years, the rapidly growing startup had evolved into a three-business organization that needed a systematic management system for its developing operations.

Teemu Tiilikainen, COO, describes that Talented consists, in principle, of very self-guided teams with a lot of ideas and enthusiasm. In selecting the management system it was important that the model would continue to support enthusiastic self-guidance whilst also bringing perseverance and focus to the work. The best thing about the OKR model has been that it clearly shows what is most important to the company's strategic objectives at any given time.

Because Talented's teams are quite autonomous and productive, they have been able to define their own Objectives and key results very freely. However, the key themes for the following year, such as strong international expansion, have been derived from Talented's strategy.

Planning OKR targets is not limited in any way other than they should be linked to these company-wide strategic themes.

The teams have independently developed their objectives and key results from their own operational activities. Different service units have their own starting points, and some services support expansion more than others. Some teams have defined their objectives entirely themselves; others have used an external facilitator to support them.

Once the team-specific objectives have been created, they are reviewed together with management. If management is satisfied with the objectives and they have been well aligned with the themes of the year, the team can start implementing their objectives. So far, this has worked. If the objectives are not in line with the strategic themes, a discussion with the team would be held, where the team would be able to justify and adjust their objective as necessary.

Tiilikainen emphasizes that key results are especially difficult to define. Sufficient time should also be allocated for implementing the model, planning and especially for retrospectives. The learning path is long and rocky, but very valuable. In Talented, the OKR model has brought a consistent journey from idea to implementation and reduced outliers in operations. "Is this in our OKRs?", is already part of the vernacular.]

3.4 Planning objectives in teams

There are different practices for planning objectives at a team level. These practices are influenced by both the autonomy and maturity of the teams and the organization's ability to give decision-making power to teams. One way is no better than any other, and the organization may choose a different method when they become more familiar with the OKR model, and when teams are encouraged to take more responsibility for their objectives.

There are generally three ways to align objectives on the team level across the company.
- Objectives can be cascaded from the upper level (cascade).
- Teams adapt higher-level objectives to suit their activities (alignment).
- Teams add their own objectives to top-level objectives.

Management must discuss, decide and agree on the method it wants to use to manage objectives for its organization. Let's take a closer look at the different options.

3.4.1 Handing teams the objectives

The traditional way of managing objectives is for management to plan the objectives for the entire organization, which are then cascaded into functions. In practice, we have found that many organizations use this method when getting started with the OKR model. Financial objectives may also benefit from cascading high-level objectives.

There are various exceptional situations in which the use of objectives determined solely by management may be justified. For example, different compliance projects may not allow implementation to be negotiated, it just has to be done, as specified, by the company as a whole. In this case, the use of direct objectives may be necessary.

In direct objectives, management has immense control of the situation. The sum of the objectives corresponds to the objective that management has set. In this way, each part of the organization receives a certain part of the predefined objectives to complete.

This does not, in principle, align with the OKR model as it completely lacks team autonomy, commitment to objective setting and discussion. We recommend that you reduce the number of direct objectives and increase the interpreted objectives as your organization adopts the OKR model and learns to look at its own work in relation to strategic objectives.

3.4.2 Interpreting the objectives in the team

The OKR model's approach to setting team objectives is through alignment. This means that the team carefully reads the management objectives and the objectives of the level above them and then adapts them to suit their operations and surroundings. The objectives are aligned with the level above, but what the team does in practice to support the objectives is defined by the team. The team is responsible for the means and implementation.

This creates the aligning force of the OKR model. The team does not ignore or change objectives, instead, they adapt or translate them to their own work. Meaningfulness, commitment, and autonomy arise from being able to determine which results and tasks are essential for the team.

Depending on the organization, and for inter-team dependencies, objective alignment can also be done horizontally. This means that some of the team's objectives can be derived from the objectives of other teams at the same organizational level. The team can freely take advantage of another team's objectives at the same level if they are also suitable for their own activities. Alignment can therefore take place both top-down and laterally.

In some organizations, teams can derive their objectives directly from management objectives. For example, if the goal of the level above is too moderate for the team and the team wants to stretch even further. OKR discussions can also contribute to those objectives higher up in the organization if teams say they can do better than the previous level has expected.

The way OKRs work is a two-way street. When teams adopt top-level objectives into their own objectives, they can also come up with entirely new top-level objectives, suggest changes to management's wording, demand a more ambitious target level, or provide management with a variety of other feedback on the objectives. This leads to discussions that will increase everyone's understanding of strategy, objectives and implementation.

CASE: Planning objectives directly from the company's objectives

In one company, the internal services management team had an objective of improving productivity, developing customer satisfaction in support functions and strengthening internal autonomy. All internal services units were to align their objectives to meet these objectives.

However, two units found that their initiatives better supported the company-wide objectives than the objectives of the internal services. At the company level, the objective was to improve the customer experience associated with the product being sold, increase sales in certain countries and lower costs.

These two service units found objectives in their own areas that supported the company strategy, by finding a new way to localize the product. The units aligned their objectives directly to the company level instead of the service unit.]

When aligning, the team needs to discuss top-level objectives so that it understands with certainty what they are aiming for and why. The team then workshops its own objectives that it can influence and make sense to stretch towards.

The objectives will be aligned with the upper level and approved by management, so that management can intervene if the objectives should not be aligned with the strategy. In general, however, teams may align well with objectives and surprise management with their creativity, innovation and courage.

3.4.3 Teams add objectives

Autonomous and self-guiding organizations can continue increasing freedom and responsibility-taking in the organization. During the alignment phase, most teams do not change or ignore objectives autonomously, but more advanced teams and companies may allow it. As the understanding of the OKR model grows, the strategic objectives and understanding of the impact of their own initiatives increases, teams can boldly begin to propose their own objectives that support strategic objectives.

Adding objectives means that management communicates the strategy and annual objectives to the organization, after which teams create and suggest their own objectives. If they are aligned with the strategy, work can begin. Some rules and guidelines for adding your own objectives may exist. Some of these are:

- All objectives must be derived from the level above.
- One of the five objectives can be the team's own.
- Half of the objectives can be suggested by the team.
- The team develops all its objectives by themselves.

In most cases, teams end up with a combination, where some of the objectives are precisely derived from higher-level objectives and some are the team's own. Teams often have features or activities in their daily work that are very important for the well-being and growth of the company but are not reflected in strategic objectives. That's why you should always listen carefully to your team's suggestions.

For example, a team might have a situation where customer satisfaction has fallen alarmingly low in the KPIs. It is then justified to add increasing customer satisfaction to the OKRs of that team. It may well be that strategic objectives cannot even be started until the team has first solved one of its most acute problems

3.4.4 The model develops alongside the organization

Often, when you first deploy the OKR model, management plays a larger role in setting objectives. The number of individual team objectives and autonomy increases as common understanding increases and skills improve. Trust in the teams' abilities to set their own objectives is strengthened by time and experience.

When implementing the OKR model, you should agree on how objectives are shared and created in your organization. Each organization is unique, so this must always be adapted. Organizational maturity and change velocities vary, which is why the chosen objective management model can also change as the situation develops.

Traditional	Intermediate	Autonomous
Management sets the objectives and they are distributed among operations.	Half of the objectives are aligned with the upper-level objectives; the team develops half of its objectives based on the strategy itself.	Management clarifies the strategy; teams propose objectives for management approval.

Three levels of objective management.

Planning team objectives increases team enthusiasm and ownership of the objectives. At the same time, it adds to the enthusiasm to stretch towards objectives and the likelihood that the objectives will be achieved. For this reason, management should keep quite a lot of room for negotiation and innovation regarding objectives so that people's ideas can be included among the organization's important issues.

3.5 OKR Tracking

Last, we'll focus on tracking in the OKR model. While inspiring objectives, concrete key results and careful planning can get things to a great start; regular tracking keeps the wheel turning. Companies often already have practices to track productivity and they will continue being used when implementing the OKR model. However, it is not uncommon that these practices have to be created. The OKR model requires discipline and a tight tracking cadence.

Follow-up meetings are needed to check key results, update numbers and tackle potential obstacles. In addition to the key results themselves, the confidence score is updated regularly. This score sometimes reflects progress better than key results. At the end of the period retrospectives are held where teams work together to review the past period to gather valuable information for planning the next period.

3.5.1 Tracking cadence in OKR

The tracking cadence of the OKR model is strongly linked to the cadence of planning and implementation. The role of tracking is just as important, if not more important, than the role of planning. When you add tracking to your timeline, it looks like this.

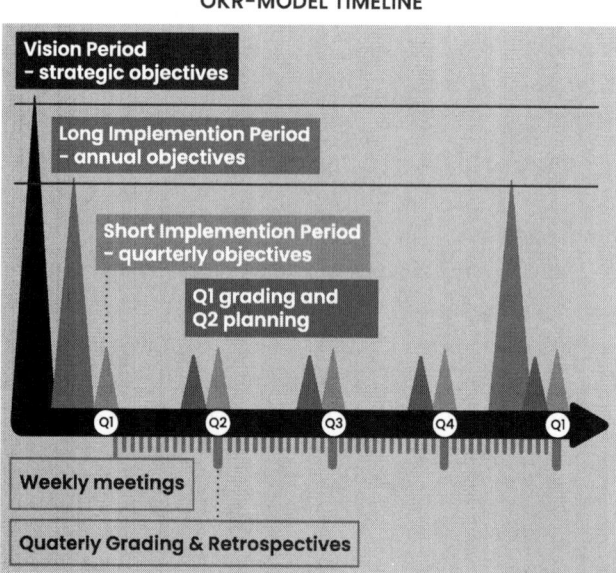

OKR-MODEL TIMELINE

- Vision Period – strategic objectives
- Long Implementation Period – annual objectives
- Short Implementation Period – quarterly objectives
- Q1 grading and Q2 planning
- Q1, Q2, Q3, Q4, Q1
- Weekly meetings
- Quaterly Grading & Retrospectives

Typical timeline in the OKR model.

A team that works according to the OKR model meets weekly to view the quarter's progress. They will discuss key results and check how they are coming along and what has happened in the past week. In rare cases, changes can be followed up on biweekly if there is a good reason for it, for instance, geographical necessities.

However, the team should ideally meet weekly to manage and advance daily work related to the OKRs. As we have already mentioned on a couple of occasions, updating the OKRs should be combined with other mechanisms of steering work, such as a classic weekly meeting. A separate OKR meeting is a bad idea because objectives must not be separate from other work management.

The OKR model is not designed to create a situation in which objectives created at the start of the are only reviewed a year later when it is stated that nothing has happened, or that the direction has changed dramatically during the year. OKRs are always present in discussions, work planning and prioritization. This also allows teams to analyze and implement their initiatives that contribute to the company's most important objectives every week.

3.5.2 What happens in the weekly meeting?

The most important tool for tracking progress is the weekly meeting. Before joining the weekly meeting, team members update the key results and confidence scores. The confidence score is described in more detail in the next section, but in short, it indicates the team's confidence in the achievability of the key result.

During tracking, the team, led by the team leader, will review the objectives and key results that have obstacles, challenges, or prioritization needs. In addition, the team celebrates objectives that are progressing well and rejoice in any successes. Some teams may review all key results if it is necessary to share information about each objective with the entire team. In general, only items that need attention are focused on.

If major problems surface during the review, a separate time slot will be set for them. Yes/no decisions and issues that can be resolved immediately are dealt with during the weekly meeting. If there is a more complex problem that requires discussion such as prioritization, organization, resourcing or reassessment it is necessary to set aside a separate session for the matter.

A weekly meeting should be a smooth and quick affair that does not consume too much of the entire team's productive time. Retrospectives or experience sharing occasions should be attended by the whole team and should be allocated sufficient time. These occasions strengthen common learning and team spirit.

3.5.3 The confidence score as an indicator of progress

Alongside key result achievement progress, the confidence score is also tracked. As its name suggests, the confidence score indicates how confident team members are in achieving the key result on time.

Often, the confidence score indicates the probability of the success of the implementation period more than the numerical value of the key result. This is because the key results are end-result-oriented. They do not deal with progress, only the final outcome (the only exception would be in section 2.3.6 *Pro-*

gress can be a key result). The final results are often realized only towards the end of the quarter.

If you only look at the key result and how it progresses, it may appear in the early stages of the quarter that nothing is moving at all. In reality, a lot of work has gone into the key results. For example, the key result may be an improvement in the customer satisfaction survey and from the beginning of the quarter, teams have started to implement development projects that improve customer satisfaction. However, the result of the query itself comes with a delay.

In this case, the confidence score is an excellent indicator of the real situation. When the team knows that they have done the right things and trust that the key result will proceed as desired, the confidence score will also be high. Maintaining high confidence is more important than measuring if the key result of the quarterly objective is progressing with a twelfth of the total each week. Steady progression is often practically impossible.

The confidence score is first and foremost a communication about the work situation. Its purpose is to show progress and also to make problems visible. That's why, in a weekly meeting, sharing bad news is as beneficial as sharing good news. Not sharing or even punishing bad news can lead to hiding mistakes and problems.Just like how failing to meet objectives should not be punished because it prevents people from daring to stretch;.

When the team shares bad news in time, it is still possible to adapt to the situation. One can think about what to do if the objectives are not achieved. Help can be brought in to get objectives done. It is also possible to prioritize which part of the objective should be focused on.

The confidence score answers the question: "How likely are we to achieve this key result by the end of the quarter?" The scale can be determined by the company itself. In most cases, the scale is similar to that in *Section 2.3.8 Key results demonstrate progress*, the 1-10 scale.

Many OKR software solutions have included the key result confidence score as an out-of-the-box feature. Some vendors talk about status rather than confidence, "what is the current situation or value of the key result in relation to the plan". The latter is a more KPI-like situational review, and the first is more a debate-driven and forward-looking assessment.

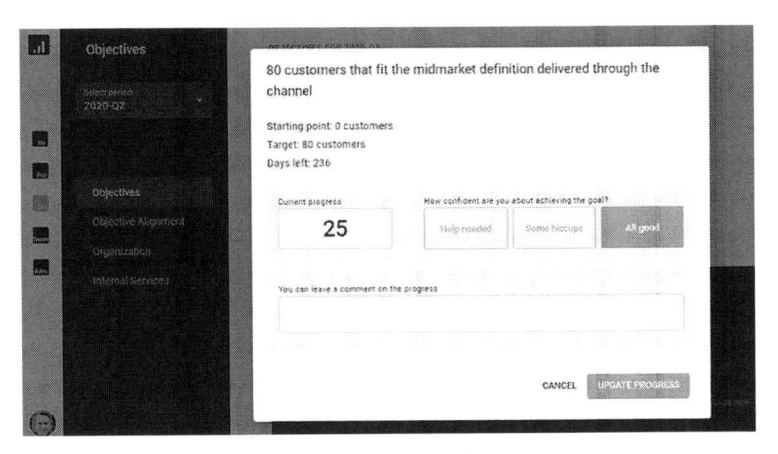

Setting the confidence score in Tangible Growth

3.5.4 End-of-month activities

The rhythm of the OKR model does not really involve monthly tracking; the answer to what is done at the end of the month could simply be "nothing different". Weekly tracking ensures that at the end of the month we know where the objectives and key results are heading. The end of the month is not a significant moment in the OKR model, until the end of the third month.

Companies tend to have other well-established monthly rituals. At the end or beginning of a month, sales figures, performance tables and KPI values are viewed and monthly meetings are held. It is not necessary to stop with these as we recommend that the OKR model's status should be integrated into these events as well.

This ensures that OKRs stay on everyone's mind at all times and are intertwined with all the other things that the company is tracking. Employees are better suited to assess the consequences of their activities when each report also shows the current OKR situation. In addition, conflicts between for example, KPI metrics or sales results and OKR targets are quickly detected.

3.5.5 Moving from one quarter to the next

The end of the quarter is a significant moment in the OKR model. It involves three very important steps. First, the key results are graded and the outcome of the past quarter is checked. Then, the lessons learned and analysis of the identified shortcomings and strengths in operations are collected.Finally, the objectives and key results of the next quarter are planned.

In section 2.3.8, we have discussed grading the key results. Grading is carried out throughout the quarter; progress is assessed every week. There are many different models for grading, but the clearest and simplest of these is Google's traffic light model, as described in Section 2.3.8. If less than a third of the key result has been achieved, then it has been poorly realized and the color is red. If more than one-third but less than two-thirds of the key result has been achieved, then it is reasonably realized and the color is yellow. If, in turn, more than two-thirds of the key result has been realized, then it is well-realized and the color is green.

At the end of the quarter, the final grades are given and the situation will be examined. If all the key results are in green, it is worth asking whether the objectives and key results had enough stretch in them. If everything is red, we need to look at what prevented the objectives from being achieved. This learning and data collection phase is related to the retrospective, which we will discuss in the next chapter.

Once the organization has analyzed the past quarter and collected the lessons learned, it's time to plan the next one. At the start of the new quarter, the objectives of the previous quarter are assessed. New key results will be planned for incomplete objectives. New objectives are planned to replace those that have been achieved. The planning of the following quarter follows the same principles as the first, so the cadence resumes to sections 3.3 *Planning short-term for a quarter* and 3.4. *Planning objectives in teams*.

In addition, at the turn of the quarter, management will review the quarterly results in relation to annual objectives. This may also be done more frequently depending on the management team, for example monthly, weekly,. At the latest, end of quarter, management assesses:

- Whether the annual objectives still support the strategy, or whether something has changed.
- Whether the annual targets will be achieved at this rate.
- Whether implementation should be adjusted somehow, or whether the organization can plan the next quarterly objectives as they did the previous quarter.
- What learning and skills the organization needs to support operations.
- How processes and operations can be developed to make the OKR model work even better.

In this way, information generated by the OKR model helps to implement the strategy and drive the organization's objectives. The quarterly review will provide a critical and realistic assessment of the company's strategy and allow taking the necessary corrective measures in time. This also leaves less room for excuses at the end of the year.

3.5.6 Retrospectives

Retrospectives or reflection meetings are an integral part of the end of each implementation cycle – and a prerequisite for planning the next period. Teams organize a retrospective at the end of each quarter. Before the new implementation period begins, the team sits down and looks at the past period to learn, develop and improve the OKR model.

There are two separate issues to deal with in a retrospective. The first is viewing the objectives of the period and the results achieved during the period. The second is the company's systemic behavior and function around the OKR model.

First, the team and the company as a whole review the planned objectives and the results achieved during the period. It is a good idea to consider objectives and results from at least the following aspects:
- How well was each objective achieved? Why?
- If there is a discrepancy, what is the reason?
- Were the objectives too easy or too difficult?
- What can we learn from the situation?
- Who should I give feedback to?
- Are the objectives still relevant?

In addition, organizational behavior and functioning around the OKR model will be examined. This can be clarified, for example, by:
- How often were the key results updated compared to how often they were meant to be updated?
- Were the people present at the OKR meetings?
- How well did the alignment of the objectives go?
- Did objectives or key results change during the period?
- Did the focus stay on the objectives, or was there something "more important" elsewhere?
- How do we change our behavior for the next period?

Depending on the size of your organization, it's a good idea to document. at the very least, the team lessons from the period and how the team's activities will change in the future. In addition, it may also be justified to compile proposed changes based on what was learned at an organizational level.

An external facilitator can even be used for retrospectives. Especially if retrospectives are not something that the organization is not already familiar with, additional support may be good. However, with time, the team leader's skills grow, and retrospectives can be arranged within the team. Here are a few tips on organizing a good retrospective:

- Participants are given enough time to think about the answers to the questions first by writing in silence. You can also ask them to do this prior to the retrospective.
- Learning can be collected through post-it notes placed on a timeline or by theme.
- Everyone gets their turn to speak about their insights, experiences, and lessons. At this stage, interruptions, justifications, and explanations from others are forbidden.
- The team leader ensures that the retro focuses on the problem and prevents finger-pointing inside or outside the team.
- The root cause can be found, for example, by asking "why?" five times. By diving deep enough, you can discover the hidden, problematic structures and invisible causes.
- During the summary phase, the leader ensures that the content of the issues raised has not been altered by the summarization.

3.6 Summary and what's next

This chapter was all about planning, implementation, and tracking in the OKR model. The whole chapter can be summed up with the following picture.

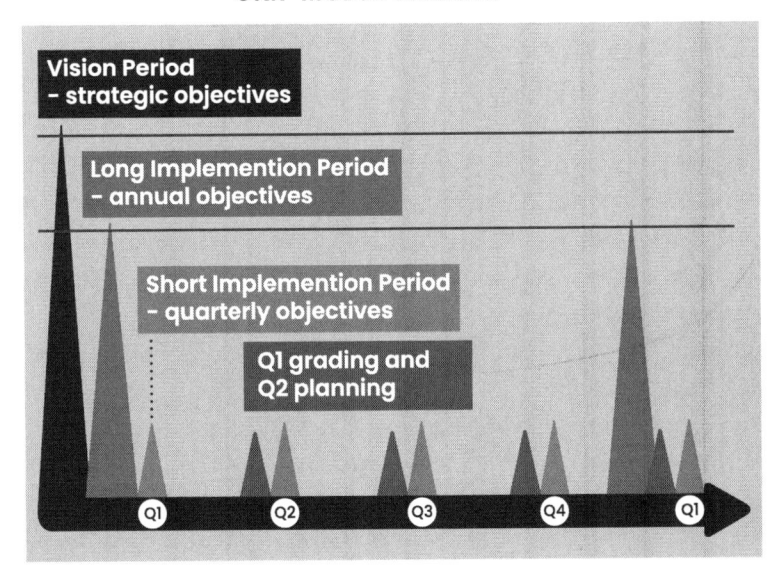

OKR-MODEL TIMELINE

Vision Period – strategic objectives

Long Implemention Period – annual objectives

Short Implemention Period – quarterly objectives

Q1 grading and Q2 planning

Q1   Q2   Q3   Q4   Q1

Typical timeline of the OKR model.

At this stage, you, the reader, will hopefully have an overall view of the vision period, i.e. the strategic objectives, the long implementation period, i.e. annual objectives and the short implementation period, i.e. quarterly objectives. In addition, we hope we have managed to stress that, depending on the company, the long and short implementation periods may be very different from a year and a quarter.

This chapter also explained how often the objectives and key results of the OKR model are tracked and updated. Although by page count, planning was discussed more than tracking, the truth is that even the best plan is not a finished product. Tracking is absolutely crucial in actually ensuring that objectives progress amid the rush and chaos of everyday life.

The following chapter describes the prerequisites and steps for an OKR model deployment project. We will go into detail on things that need to be done first to make the OKR model viable. After the fourth chapter, everyone can roll up their sleeves and take action – although you might also want to read Chapter Five to help you manage expectations and successfully lead a change project.

4 OKR IMPLEMENTATION

When implementing the OKR model, the most important thing to do is get started. To avoid *analysis paralysis*, it is paramount to just get something done. Nothing can be improved unless something exists to improve and develop further. It's okay to just get going!

Objective and key result writing can only truly be learned by writing them for your own organization. OKRs will become more accurate as you gain experience with each quarter. You will learn to notice what does and does not work and learn how to make what works even better. Getting started is also important because even though learning OKRs is a long process, you are generating value by learning from the very first steps you take.

Implementing the OKR model usually follows this progression

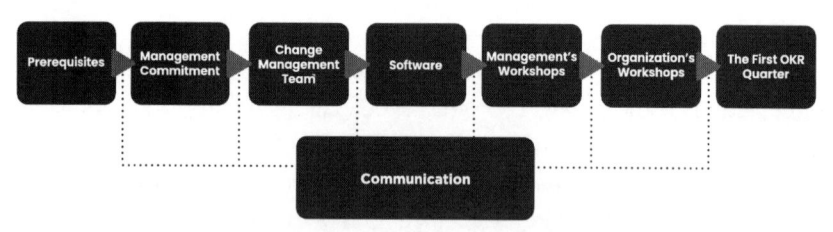

```
Prerequisites → Management Commitment → Change Management Team → Software → Management's Workshops → Organization's Workshops → The First OKR Quarter
                                                    ↓
                                              Communication
```

Typical progression in implementing the OKR model.

1. **Investigating readiness.**
2. **Decision on implementation and management commitment.**
3. First communication to the organization about the objectives and process.
4. **Choosing an internal champion, a possible consultant and creating the transformation project team.**
5. Communicating choices and the schedule of deployment to the organization
6. **Choosing the software (or making a decision not to use software)**
7. The first workshops with management and pilot teams that produce the initial versions of the OKRs.

8. Communicating progress.
9. Workshop for finalizing the first management OKRs.
10. Communicating the first alignment workshops.
11. Defining team-level objectives
12. Starting the first OKR quarter.

We discussed in the previous chapter how the objectives are derived from the strategy, as well as the basics of planning. These methods are used in sections 7, 9 and 11 of the deployment. In this chapter, we will go through points 1, 2, 4 and 6 which are in bold above, which are the prerequisites and deployment steps from a project, system and organizational perspective . In addition, we are going through consolidating priority lists, which is considered an advanced topic.

In the next chapter, we will discuss people, culture and communication (steps 3, 5, 8, and 10). Both aspects are important to move smoothly into functioning OKRs. Remember, even if you stumble at the start, you are still making progress. The most important thing is to get started!

4.1 Prerequisites and management commitment

At this stage, the organization initiating the implementation of the OKR model should be able to answer the following questions on a general level:
- What is the OKR model?
- What does it do and why is it worth implementing?
- How are the objectives and key results created?
- How are OKRs planned and how are they tracked?
- How are OKRs reflected in the everyday life of an organization?

Once you have the answers to these questions, you have a sufficient understanding within the company to launch the actual implementation project.

The first step of implementation is to look at requirements within the company. At this time, it is also necessary to ensure that management is truly prepared to commit to the implementation of OKRs. This seems obvious, but we have seen and heard of several failed OKR projects, where management has been excited about the idea at first but not actually committed to what it takes to finish the project.

4.1.1 Prerequisites and What it takes

Based on our own experience and that gathered from others, the adoption of the OKR model requires four things from the organization:

1. The company has a strategy.
2. The management of the company has the right attitude.
3. The maturity level of the company has been identified.
4. The company has enough time to implement the change.

1. The company has a strategy

As mentioned more than once in the previous chapter, the company must have a strategy or at least a rough draft, which will then be developed further with the help of OKRs. A finalized or near-finished strategy is a prerequisite for the adoption of the OKR model since the OKR model is not a tool for creating the strategy, but a tool for tracking the implementation and progress of the strategy.

OKRs help you bring the strategy into everyday work. When an organization has a strategy, it is used as a source for the objectives and key results that the organization begins to implement. Unless you have a strategy, the OKR model will not be able to guide the organization towards a desired strategic change.

2. The management of the company has the right attitude

Another prerequisite for the successful implementation of the OKR model is the attitude of management. Section *4.1.3 Management commitment is vital* goes into more detail on how and in what way management should engage with the adoption of the OKR model and with the related organizational and cultural changes.

Management must be prepared to give more decision-making power to its staff than before. It is very difficult to implement the OKR model in a hierarchical and strongly top-down organization. However, it becomes possible if management is willing to change and let go of power.

3. The maturity level of the company has been identified

The third prerequisite is being able to identify the maturity level of the organization in order to know how much autonomy and responsibility can be given to teams. The adoption of the OKR model is modified according to the level of maturity in the organization. If the organization is accustomed to objectives being given by management, it cannot suddenly be expected to be able to take ownership of objectives - there will be a learning curve in regards to this behavior.

In these cases, the confidence and belief that they have both the power and the ability to determine their objectives grows slowly. For an organization that is accustomed to creating its own objectives and having them approved by management, moving to the OKR model is not a massive change and may happen quite quickly.

4. The company has enough time

The fourth prerequisite is that the organization has sufficient time to implement the model. Implementing the OKR model requires at least a quarter for the easiest cases and most likely 4 to 5 quarters. Actual results, lessons and improvements will not be observable until six months after the start.

Discussions and workshops related to launching the model itself and setting objectives also require significant time. Often implementation projects fail because sufficient resources are not allocated.

Before starting the implementation, it is good for management to deliberate on the following:
- Are we ready to commit to this?
- Are we really willing to engage the organization in decisions?
- Are we willing to allocate enough time for the implementation?
- Is the strategy ready enough?
- Has the maturity of the organization been taken into account?

When the answers to all of the above are "yes", the prerequisites for implementing the model are all there.

4.1.2 Why is the OKR model implemented?

One of the prerequisites to successfully implementing the OKR model is to know why the OKR model is being implemented in the first place. This sounds obvious, but it doesn't always feel obvious. There is a very assorted set of reasons and explanations for why the model is being implemented. These may include, "The boss happened to hear an inspiring presentation.", "The competition uses it too.", "Google does it." and "A business influencer praised a particular book in a book club."

There's nothing bad about getting excited. Successful projects require at least some of the people to be excited about them and see their value. But the

value is not transferred unless the people who communicate it know how to answer the simplest and most annoying question: Why? Why-questions may include the following:
- Why is this important for our organization?
- Why does this help us move forward?
- Why should I go along with this?
- Why should I care?

One of the greatest work-related breakthroughs of our time is realizing the importance of meaning in work. This search for meaning increasingly determines our choices. We want work that matters, as Daniel Pink explains in his book *Drive: The Surprising Truth About What Motivates Us*. According to Pink, the purpose of work is one of three factors driving our motivation.

Simon Sinek also emphasized the longing for meaning in his book *Start With Why*. According to Sinek, every company needs to be clear about why the company exists. Those who can justify their existence succinctly and get customers and employees engaged in an excitable way.

In the same way, longing for relevance also applies to internal transformations, such as the implementation of the OKR model. A clear, bright and succinct answer is needed to the question "Why will the OKR model be implemented?".

Since the adoption of the OKR model requires changes in culture, practices and processes, the reason for the change must be good enough - otherwise, nothing will happen.

Some examples of answers for justifying the OKR model:
- Ambientia: So that every person is connected to the new strategy.
- Talented: So that everyone knows what's important right now and what you can say no to.
- Happy or Not: So that investors can monitor the activities of the company.
- Nixu: So that we are better able to monitor strategic developments.

As you might guess, the answer varies quite a lot between different companies. Different things are relevant to different companies and their employees. There is also often more than one reason.

From the very beginning, the reasons must be clear and they should be relevant to the staff. It doesn't matter if it sounds like a good reason to others, as long as your own people adopt it. It should be the guiding light of communication throughout the implementation.

4.1.3 Leadership commitment is essential

Once management has clearly defined for itself why the OKR model is being brought into the company, it must commit to its decision seriously and earnestly. Management engagement means at least the following things:
- Management will jointly decide to change the management system and align the OKR model with the current operations.
- Management chooses a project owner from its ranks.
- Management selects a consultant from outside the organization or trains an internal OKR specialist.
- Management understands that it takes a long time to get results and won't give up even if things sometimes seem difficult.
- Management commits to changing its behavior and habits.
- Management will provide funding for the project.

As deployment of the OKR model will take some time and there are likely to be tough times, the commitment to the OKR model from the management team needs to be long enough for the results to start showing. Any change on this scale is likely to encounter problems and so the management team needs to be consistent in their work and engage in dialogue with teams.

As stated before, the training period for the OKR model is a quarter. After three months we will gain our first experiences and discuss them. In our experience, three to five quarters, or about one year, are required for significant results.

Management's commitment is also a sign of daring to change. One essential change for management is that it puts itself under radical transparency - the objectives of management and how they come to fruition are there for all to see.

In the past, it may have been possible for the strategy to be communicated to the organization once, and if for any reason it had failed, it happened silently. The failure may have been explained in hindsight, for example, by the situation or customers having changed or by not having enough time.

After OKR implementation, hindsight is not required , since OKRs are being tracked throughout the organization through the year. The OKR model requires action and communication about hindrances if objectives are not progressing. Objectives in the OKR model are monitored by everyone, and often you can find people in the organization who follow them closely. This helps with transparency - a net positive.

There is one more prerequisite for the success of implementing the OKR model, and it may require a change in attitude from management. That is the acceptance of failures with objectives — including management's own objectives. Management may need, perhaps for the first time, to accept failures in both its own and others' activities.

It may take significant practice before managers can relate to failures in a way that maintains psychological safety and encourages teams to pick themselves up and try again. The end result, however, makes it worth persevering.

Case Flowa: What does management commitment look like?

It's easy to say that "management is committed" or "I am committed." But what does commitment actually mean? The co-founder of the consulting and software development company Flowa, Coach **Antti Kirjavainen,** has seen several organizations go through, and been involved in a wide range of transformation processes. Kirjavainen says that management commitment primarily means investing time, as that is management's main currency. A hallmark of committed leadership is providing time and the leader's willingness to have a dialogue.

For the adoption of the OKR model to be successful, management should talk to people about objectives — and the reasons behind them. Often, a 45-minute roadshow with slides and five minutes of interaction is enough. It is paramount that leaders are involved in the dialogue. An external consultant in charge of implementation is a convenient helper, but people need to feel that they have been listened to by the management of their own organization.

In a dialogue, the employees are listened to and their ideas and expertise can genuinely influence management's objectives. It's a two-way street. In the OKR model, things are done together, which can feel foreign to many organizations .A committed leadership team will put themselves in a position where they can speak with experts on equal footing. It can be scary and illuminating and takes courage and daring.

Committed management is also willing to share more than they did in the past. For a company to be able to determine its own objectives autonomously, management must make the information needed to interpret the objectives readily available. Without proper context and a shared environment, objectives are impossible to plan and align.

The final sign of management engagement is confidence that the best outcome will always eventually emerge when things are done collaboratively — even if at first glance, it seems that things are not going in the planned direction. In these situations, more information sharing, open discussion and a common understanding of the situation are required. But if management pulls the plug and takes the reins after initial adversity, then the organization was not truly committed to the objectives and operations.

Kirjavainen stresses that engagement is a prerequisite for giving the OKR model a real chance to come to fruition. Committed management is willing to put effort into making sure the model works.

4.1.4 Checklist of required skills

The last precursor to implementation is to check the company's competencies. The implementation of the OKR model requires certain skills that a company should acquire or contract for the duration of the implementation period. These skills must, in particular, be found in the deployment team, which we will talk about in the next section.

The implementation of the OKR model requires that the team performing it has:

- the ability to facilitate workshops and organize results-centric meetings
- basic understanding of OKR theory
- basic understanding of the target setting and the business of the company
- understanding how to create a smart strategy
- competence in quantifying things and competence in measuring
- project management basics and the ability to break things down (Work Breakdown Structure, WBS)
- discipline, reflection skills, and resilience
- the ability to work backwards from the desired results
- resilience and acceptance that this is a long path
- permission to plan and implement

Of course, these skills will be honed during the project, but consider that without these skills the project will likely only succeed through luck, if it happens to succeed at all. It is time to launch the project only when everyone is clear on why you are doing this, the prerequisites for implementation have been reviewed, management is committed and the know-how is in place.

4.2 The implementation project

The size of the project depends on the size of the company. In some companies, the change is small and the project is just one project among others. The bigger and older the company, the bigger the change will be, along with the initial chaos from adopting the OKR model. Regardless of the size of the company, there are three things involved in the transformation.

First, the company needs a transformation project team, that is, a team that concretely manages, tracks and ensures the successful implementation of the OKR model. Typically it has at least three people, but should only have enough team members to be capable of running workshops together. If the size of the transformation project team swells, efficiency will suffer. The role of the team and the duties of the team members will be discussed in section 4.2.1 Change management organization.

Secondly, a necessary element for success is the internal champion or OKR specialist. The internal champion plays the most important role in the transformation project team. This person brings excitement and competence to the whole organization. The role of the internal champion will be discussed in Section 4.2.2 *Internal champion or OKR expert*.

Finally the organization needs a system in which OKRs are recorded and maintained. The system can be anything from a whiteboard and post-it tags to sophisticated and complex OKR software. There are plenty of options to suit every organization.

This is it in its entirety and simplicity. The company only needs a team, an internal champion with sufficient OKR expertise and a method to collect OKRs. After this, the workshops can begin.

4.2.1 Change management team

Changes don't happen by themselves. They always involve friction and unlearning. Change also involves a lot of work that someone has to do. This is also the case with implementing the OKR model. For this work, a transformation project team is required, a team that drives the OKR model into practice together with the teams.

Project team duties include
- communicate all the different stages and progress of the OKR project until the end of the implementation.

- serve as a link between teams and management and collect important feedback.
- address any challenges that arise and seek solutions to them in cooperation with management and teams.
- report on the progress to the management team regularly.
- run management workshops and OKR planning.
- help teams to run their first workshops and align objectives with the management objectives.
- help with the implementation of the system to record and maintain OKRs.
- answer thousands of questions patiently.

The team has at least three members:

1. an internal champion - the OKR expert
2. a committed management representative and sponsor
3. a staff representative

The OKR expert is the most important person on the project team. They have to have sufficient OKR skills and be able to transfer and teach the necessary skills to the rest of the organization.

The management sponsor is the person who owns the implementation of the OKR model in the management team. They are, in IT industry terms, a *product owner* who is ultimately responsible for the progress and success of the project. The management sponsor has three essential functions. First, the management representative ensures that the rest of management stays committed to implementing the model and believes in its value. Secondly, they also ensure that the funding for the project stays secure. Thirdly, the management sponsor, through personal communication, makes sure that the rest of the company understands how important and desired this change is.

A staff representative is an important source of information. They know the everyday life of the company and the pains and fears of the employees. They know how to raise essential issues for consideration even before they are presented to all staff, thereby helping to navigate potential pitfalls. In addition, They are the person other employees often share realistic views that would be difficult to share with a management representative or the internal champion, who is excited about the OKR model.

In addition to these three, there may be other experts on the project team whose expertise will be helpful when implementing the model. We recommend keeping the team at a moderate size in order to focus more on the deployment itself than on managing the team, internal communication, and team coordination.

4.2.2 The Internal champion - the OKR expert

A key member of the project team is the internal champion. The internal champion is an active and self-guided person. They are knowledgeable about the OKR model, excited about it and want to help the company adopt it. The internal champion is an OKR expert who can present their case and inspire others. Therefore, we prefer to use the term internal champion rather than OKR expert, as mere understanding is not enough. The internal champion has a vital role to play as a generator of enthusiasm and a catalyst of change.

The internal champion must be experienced in OKRs because their mission is to train the entire organization to understand and use the OKR model. To get the support needed to take the OKR model into their team's everyday life, the internal champion must be able to teach things in concrete terms and be able to facilitate various workshops, including management workshops.

To succeed, the internal champion must have enough time, especially in the early stages of the project. They must also be reasonably free to decide their own working hours so that the project does not suffer scheduling problems. There may be more than one internal champion in the project, and the bigger the organization, the more likely it is for each business area to have its own internal champion.

It's probably a good thing if the internal champion isn't a management representative as it is often difficult for employees to approach and ask questions directly to management. The internal champion must be easily approachable and also have an open, fast, and functional conversational channel to the management of the company. This is so they can get the decisions, answers and approvals they need from management quickly.

The internal champion may also be an external consultant with experience in implementing the OKR model in other organizations. The upside of a consultant is they can see things from an outside perspective and can question the business's activities more directly than someone coming from inside the company. In addition, practical experience with other implementation projects will be helpful when a new project is launched.

The downside of a consultant is that the company is — at least initially — dependent on an external resource. To ensure a successful transformation, the consultant should train in-house specialists to help with the deployment and to ultimately make themselves redundant. In the long run, success with the OKR model should not be dependent on outside assistance. Everything needed to manage OKRs should be within the company. The best result is often obtained by finding an enthusiastic internal champion in the company, who is then coached by an external OKR expert.

Once the internal champion or internal champions are selected, the decision is communicated to the entire company so people know who to turn to and who to ask questions. The whole transformation project team should be announced at the same time. Employees should know who has the mandate to hold workshops, convene teams and promote the project independently.

CASE: Ambientia's internal champion served as OKR Champion

When the OKR model was implemented at Ambientia, an OKR Champion was named to work shoulder to shoulder with the management representative who owned the project. The OKR Champion's role was part-time, as there were other responsibilities. Early on, about one-third of his working time was spent on OKR implementation.

First, an external trainer trained the management team and the OKR Champion in OKR. The first workshops were jointly organized by the OKR Champion and the management representative. The champion took over the project after that. They trained teams and individuals selected by management to use the OKR model and engaged with the teams. They also trained the teams in the use of Tangible Growth software.

The OKR Champion and the owner of the project rolled out the project by both reporting progress on the company's intranet and discussion channels. They answered questions,participated in discussions and in addition, the OKR topic was added to other management messages, such as CEO communications.

At Ambientia, the OKR Champion spent about 150 working hours during 2019, as well as organized around 15 different workshops for teams. All of Ambientias's 200 employees each spent a few hours on the implementation as part of the teams' normal management practices. Ambientia's management felt that the initial effort as a whole was clearly a good investment.

Case: Futurice's internal champion created his own OKR materials

In January 2019, **Viljami Väisänen** was chosen as Futurice's internal champion. His role has been a mix of internal champion and staff representative. He has driven the implementation of the OKR model in close collaboration with company management and in particular **Olli-Pekka Germany** (Global Head of Human Care), one of the original sponsors of the OKR model at Futurice. A formal project team with more people has not been needed so far.

As an internal champion, Väisänen has noticed that the implementation of the OKR model requires stamina and repetition, like any other transformation project. Since Futurice is a global company with more than 600 employees, the early stages have been full of work. Väisänen has scaled his efforts by making easily approachable instruction materials to support implementation.

Because people are hungry for quick and easy information, it is common to find information via Google. With the OKR model being very context-specific, sponsored search content often tends to overgeneralize the subject. In the worst-case scenario, search results provide incorrect information that does not align with the company's own approach to the OKR model. This creates unnecessary fear and confusion.

For the internal champion, acting as an interpreter between "I found this by googling" and the company approach is critical. Therefore, from the start, Futurice's internal champion sought to create easily absorbable content for internal use, while answering classic questions such as, "Why us? What? How? When? Why should I be interested?"

Somewhere along the way, the *OKRs Guidebook by Futurice* was created. It was initially utilized in Futurice's internal training and later, with customers. After the first 100 or so people had been trained face-to-face on OKR basics, Väisänen also made a video training course. The course consists of snappy videos, each a few minutes long.

Taking advantage of fast-paced short videos has saved time in implementation, as Väisänen has been able to answer frequently asked questions with clear videos instead of repeating the answers continuously. The running theme of the videos has been how the OKR model has been applied to Futurice's culture and values.]

4.2.3 The OKR journey – Futurice case study

Futurice has been consulting in IT for 20 years. They have operations in several countries, with eight offices and employ over 600 members of staff. Futurice has delivered more than 3000 projects and the corporation also includes Aito.ai, Columbia Road, and Tentimes.

Futurice's OKR journey began with an enthusiastic idea in December 2018. The decision to trial the OKR model was promptly made, and in January 2019, Viljami Väisänen was chosen to lead the project as an internal champion.

The objective of adopting the OKR model was defined as:
"increase internal

1. alignment
2. Focus, and
3. prioritization

to achieve common objectives in accordance with company values."

The aim was to increase the realization of the strategy while strengthening Futurice's already powerful culture and values at the same time.

In keeping with Futurice's trial culture, the OKR model was implemented through experimentation. The first OKR experiment took place over a few weeks in January and February with two small teams. A former Google middle management employee served as a sparring partner. The start of the year also included diligent and in-depth study of the OKR model, as well as the first versions of the internal instruction book and training.

In March 2019, after the first trial, it was time to implement a more systematic OKR round. The second quarter of the year included more than 30 people in the process. All were trained, coached and instructed in creating OKRs. At this point, OKRs were still recorded in Google Sheets.

In May 2019, Futurice ventured from the testing phase to the deployment phase, as feedback gathered from those involved in the testing phase was encouragingly positive. The CEO told the company that from January 2020 onwards the goal is to run the company using the OKR model. During June, the first enterprise-level OKR targets were set for the second half of the year, along with quarterly OKRs for two countries and multiple teams. It was also noted that after the holidays, a big chunk of the lessons had been forgotten and that there was a need to repeat the message tenaciously.

A lot was learned during the first practice rounds. Based on feedback, OKRs helped several teams in prioritizing and increasing transparency. In particular, simultaneous planning and having difficult prioritization discussions on a common schedule were perceived as valuable. Several of the employees also found that uninterrupted work during the quarter was beneficial. Many also welcomed the idea that during the quarter, generally no changes to the objectives are made.

Positive experiences encouraged Futurice to continue, although resistance to change and negative experiences also occurred. For example, they learned that in consulting organizations, those employees whose entire working time is spent in client projects and therefore, advancing the client's objectives could find it difficult to combine the objectives of the client and their own company.

This encouraged formulating objectives to make them as inclusive as possible and reachable by those doing customer work. However, the main target audience of the OKR model was teams that do not only do client projects.

In the fall of 2019, new countries and teams were introduced to the OKR model. At the same time, the tracking system was moved from Google Sheets to SaaS-based OKR software. Betterworks was selected as the software and has served Futurice well. The OKR cadence began to quietly become established in Futurice's activities.

By the turn of the 2019-2020 year, all core teams in the internal objective setting, more than 120 people, had been inducted into the OKR program. In many teams, the OKR model was perceived as having improved the focus of work and increased communication between teams. Many employees have adopted a continuous development attitude towards the OKR model. Prioritizing and managing project counts have also improved along the way.

Some teams have adopted OKRs and related tracking with ease as part of their working practices. Others have had more trouble in prioritizing and keeping the focus on the common objectives amid sudden and urgent issues. All the while, management, the internal champion and core teams have continuously reflected how communication and performance could be further developed.

With the start of the second quarter in April 2020, Futurice updated its company-level OKRs to better help the company focus on the conditions brought about by the covid-19 pandemic. Despite the exceptional circumstances, the focus is still on the chosen priorities and with OKRs, countries, international and local teams strive together to reach common objectives.

4.3 OKR-software and systems

To run the OKR model, you need a place where all the objectives and key results are collected coherently and systematically. It is good to store them in a place where everyone can see them and where they are updated regularly. Clarity, ease, and openness of the system are essential. Everyone should be able to find the information without effort so that it actually gets used.

That's where the system's mandatory requirements end. The OKR model does not require complex IT software. We have found that in a small organization a whiteboard and a pile of post-it tags work very nicely as an OKR system. We've also seen plenty of different well-functioning OKR excel sheets, as well as numerous software solutions with a lot of useful functionality built-in.

If a company has a management team and multiple other teams, or when an organization is distributed into multiple locales, the adoption of OKR software becomes justified.

With software:
- links between the top level of the organization and teams will be clearly visible
- updating and tracking key results is possible from anywhere
- the system reminds teams of key results that have not been updated

CASE: Google's OKR tools are very simple

You might think that Google, if anyone, would have a complex OKR system. In practice, Google thinks and acts differently. The company has found that the system itself is irrelevant if everyone is committed to following their own OKRs.

At Google, it is believed that for the model to work everyone needs to make OKRs their own. The bottom line is that everyone has the opportunity to influence their own OKRs. They are discussed with the team and manager. Corporate culture is built on a strong belief in individuals and what they do. Therefore at Google, the OKRs are always the objectives of the individual and not the system.

When you rely on everyone to take care of their own objectives, very simple tools are enough to be a system - everyone writes OKR targets themselves and they use software like Google Docs and Google Sheets. The OKR targets must be public and accessible to everyone.

Google wants to give the individual maximum freedom and responsibility. Good OKRs are a combination of company (*top-down*) OKRs and priorities, as well as individual (*bottom-up*) suggestions. This allows everyone to influence what they feel is important and the way they can contribute to the objectives of the company.]

4.3.1 Choosing your software

The choice of software is always based on the organization's own needs and its current situation. For this reason, universal instructions for selecting the OKR software do not exist. The choice is not made any easier when new interesting OKR software is constantly being released. Almost all OKR software solutions are cloud-based and their feature spectrum is very wide.

Generally speaking, all software contains at least the following features:

1. login with other user data sources, such as Google IDs.
2. retention of objectives and key result.,
3. horizontal and vertical linking of objectives within an organization.
4. a variety of views and dashboards for tracking progress.
5. mechanisms for grading key results.

In this chapter, we will take a closer look at Tangible Growth, Koan and Jira, as the authors have firsthand experiences with these. At the time of writing, we are aware of at least the following software options

- 7Geese [7geese.com]
- Atiim [www.atiim.com]
- BetterWorks [www.betterworks.com]
- GTmHub [gtmhub.com]
- Impraise [www.impraise.com]
- Lattice [lattice.com]
- Leapsome [leapsome.com]
- Perdoo [www.perdoo.com]
- Tight [tability.io]
- Scoro [www.scoro.com]
- Weekdone [weekdone.com]
- Workpath [www.workpath.com]

Each of them interprets OKR theory slightly differently. In addition, each OKR software also has other features supporting the OKR model. Some incorporate strategy work, some gather data from many systems automatically, some evaluate the performance level of people and so on. Therefore, software selection is often driven by other features than the OKR work itself.

Here are a few suggestions to aid in the initial selection and then we will deep-dive into four options.
- If the organization is small, links between objectives are few and people can meet at the same office. The OKR model can be implemented with a whiteboard, excel file or post-it notes.
- If an organization's goal is to obtain key results data from many existing systems automatically, GTMHub is a potentially good solution.
- If an organization wants affordable and simple OKR software and people can commit to writing weekly reflections, KOAN is a good option.
- If a large organization needs to demonstrate the adoption of the strategy, as well as related transformational projects and deploy OKRs, Tangible Growth is a good starting point.
- If an organization wants to go fast and keep execution periods very short, Weekdone might be the right choice.
- If an organization is already using Jira and is willing to invest in configuring it to achieve baseline requirements, it is worth exploring Jira as an OKR platform.
- If an organization wants to comprehensively manage people's performance evaluations, you might want to start with BetterWorks.

It is always worthwhile comparing a few different options and asking for experiences and reviews from organizations that have implemented the OKR model. No system is perfect for everything, but many are very good at running the OKR model.

4.3.2 OKRs on a whiteboard – case study Labrox

Labrox is a Finnish industrial company working in one locale in the same office space. People meet at the office at least once a week and often on a daily basis. Objectives and key results are updated with the whole organization present. Management has done pre-work, but there are few enough teams that OKRs can be done together as a one-time effort.

In the spirit of lean methodologies, Labrox has made an effort to make all the important information visible on whiteboards and walls — not inside systems. When information is visible without having to look for it on a common, large whiteboard, people are constantly reminded and kept up-to-date on the OKRs.

At the time of writing, the company has 27 employees who are in four different teams: the management team, diagnostics (equipment), research (equipment), and production. At the company level, there are five annual objectives determined by the management team over the course of four joint workshop days on strategic objectives. Each team has 4—5 objectives for the quarter. In total, the whiteboard contains about 20 objectives with key results.

The objectives and key results are not quite perfectly in line with the OKR model, but they have served well in guiding the work and above all, they show what is important. The management team updates the information on the board on Fridays and every Monday everyone jointly takes a look at the figures, making sure that the key results have progressed, and clear any obstacles.

The advantage of the whiteboard is that everything, including dependencies and connections, is visible at once. You get the big picture of progress effortlessly. The confidence values of key results are emoticons, so a sea of cheerful faces tells you everything is fine. Serious faces, on the other hand, tell us that management needs to start looking for ways to help teams achieve their objectives.

4.3.3 Repurposing Jira– case study Ambientia

Ambientia has the Tangible Growth software in use, but in addition to this, the OKR model is also managed using Atlassian's JIRA software. There is a reasonable explanation for using two systems. Ambientia itself acts as an Atlassian consultancy and the teams wanted to test whether Jira would also work as OKR software.

Jira is used in many organizations, for instance as a ticket-management system for customer service or for managing software development. It may then make sense to use the same software to manage OKRs as well. Experience has shown that it is possible with reasonable effort to build a software system suitable for OKRs by creatively using different JIRA add-ons.

The solution is simple for OKR software. But its absolute upside is that tasks in Jira are easy to link to the company structure existing in the system already. If Jira is already in use, the solution is also relatively inexpensive.

For more information on the software, visit www.atlassian.com/software/jira

4.3.4 TG software focuses on the strategy – case study Tangible Growth

The writers are most familiar with the Tangible Growth software. Juuso is one of the founders of the company and its CEO. Henri has also used the software in the capacity of Ambientia's Chief Operating Officer.

Tangible Growth's strength is that it provides the tools to implement strategic change management within the organization on a variety of levels. The OKRs play a key role in this, but besides that, the system includes tools for increasing strategy, transformation and objective comprehension.

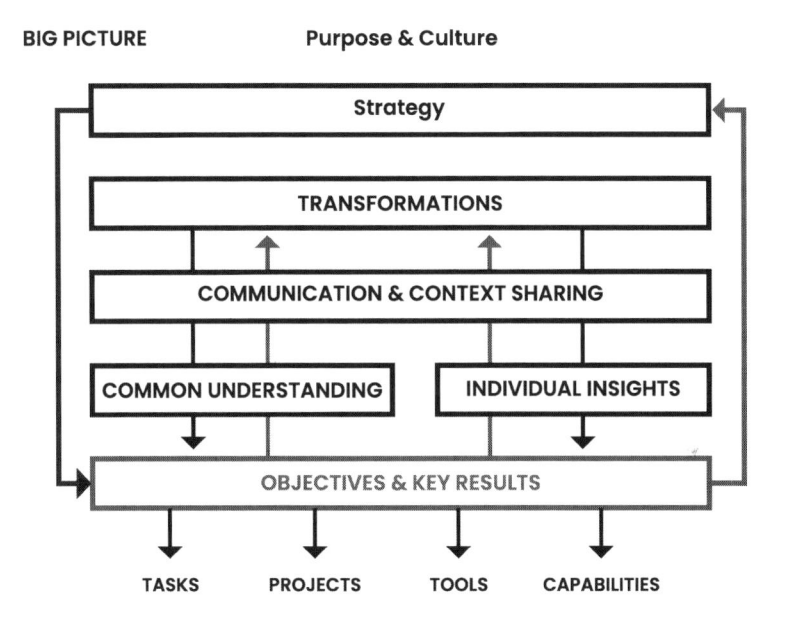

The Big Picture of Transformation: Tangible Growth

The functions of Tangible Growth are tied to defining the purpose of a company and how that purpose is communicated to employees, customers and other stakeholders. Tangible Growth places particular emphasis on real-time access to information, active context sharing and storytelling. Without breaking secrecy constraints, the organization is told why certain choices have been made, what has been considered and what open questions remain. Employees are also told how changes should be reflected in the everyday life of a customer or an employee.

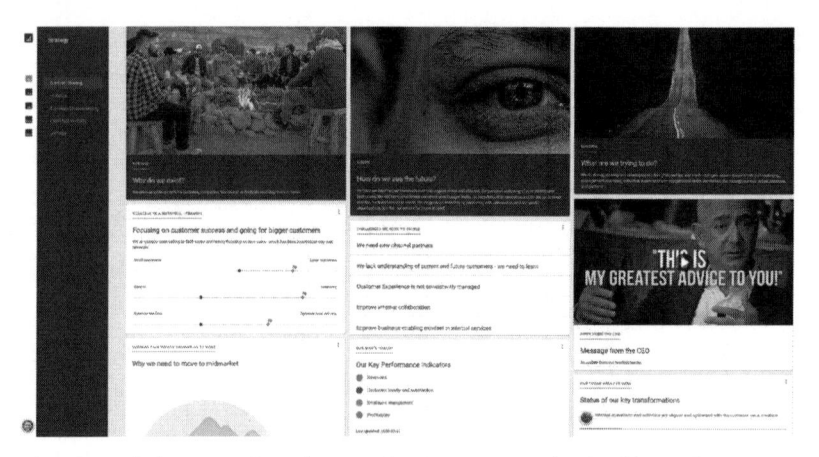

The Tangible Growth software features a variety of functions needed to manage change, such as sharing context with an organization.

Repeated communication is not enough, no matter how good it is. In an organization of 2,000 people, you will, in the worst case scenario, have 2,000 different interpretations of the strategy. Tangible Growth encourages focusing on creating a common understanding. The whole organization should take to heart at the unit and team level, how the desired changes should appear in everyday life; what needs to be clarified and what the near future will focus on. It is equally important to gather employee feedback and to find out what the change feels like from an individual's point of view, what thoughts or ideas they have and what concerns should be dispelled.

In addition to Ambientia, TG users range from international corporations to small scalable technology startups. Naturally, Tangible Growth also uses its own system. The OKR features are suitable for companies of all sizes, but the change management features truly begin to benefit organizations of more than 100 people.

The Tangible Growth software is intended to be a more wide-ranging management and transformation tool, not just for OKRs. For organizations looking solely for an OKR management tool, it may be good to investigate other options first.

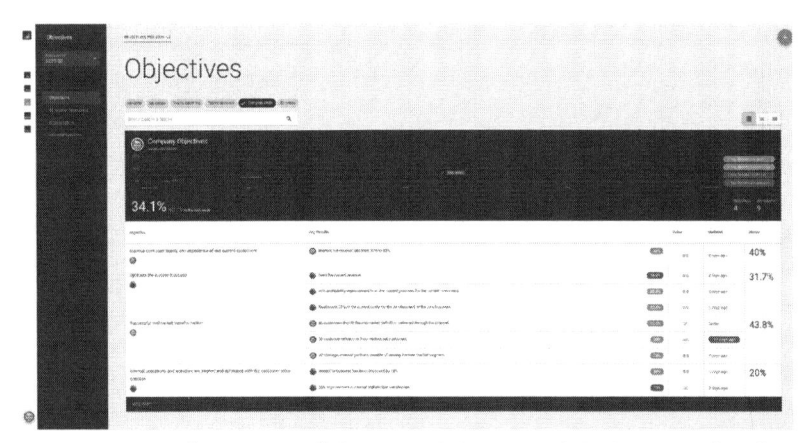

An example of how Tangible Growth has modeled enterprise-level objectives and key results.

For more information on the software, visit www.tangible-growth.com

4.3.5 Reflection and engagement with KOAN – case study Aucor

Before the company was sold to MarkkinointiAkatemia, Aucor, a Finnish digital firm, implemented its OKR management system using KOAN. KOAN is a lightweight SaaS that incorporates the basic features of OKR software. Its specialty is in the Reflections module, where employees are allowed to evaluate their own activities and provide feedback to each other.

The idea is that each company member writes a brief update in KOAN each week by answering a few selected questions, that is a reflection of the past week. The reflections look at how each individual has over the week contributed to the company's OKRs. When updates are written systematically like this every week, they accumulate a lot of information about how the company works.

In addition to writing their updates, reading others' reflections and reacting to them with comments and emojis add to the sense of cohesion within the company. In Aucor, people officially worked in three different locales and often in other remote locations as well. With reflections, people remained aware of their colleagues' work as well as the bigger picture.

With the help of reflections, Aucor's leadership also had a good overview of the company's vibe and possible issues. Thumbs and likes also serve as a two-way, light feedback channel for management and employees alike.

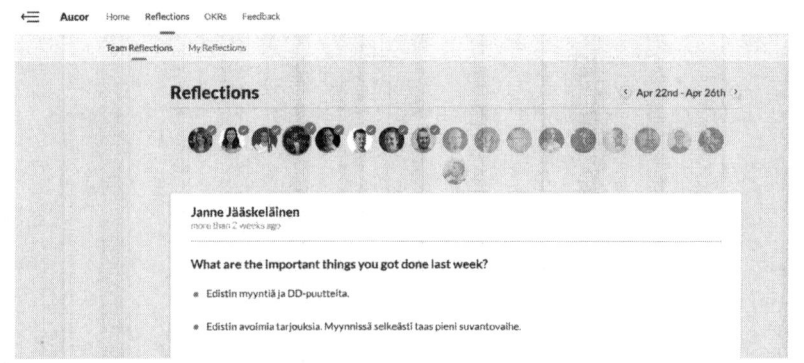

KOAN Reflections as used by Aucor.

For more information about the software, visit: www.koan.co

4.4 Integrating Management Systems

There is already some kind of management system in place in every organization. Management systems, like culture, exist whether or not actively paid attention to. Either it's formed at random or it's constructed methodically. Implementing the OKR model forces us to take a look at what kind of management system the company has and how it needs to be developed to support the OKR model and strategy implementation.

A management system consists of the agreed events, processes, and policies with which the company is managed. It can be very carefully defined, detailed in a document containing hundreds of pages and be connected to a multitude of precise quality management systems. Or alternatively, the management system may be a loose collection of habits that no one inside the company can correctly describe.

OKR is also a management system and needs to be integrated with the organization's current practices. Failure to integrate these only facilitates poor outcomes.

4.4.1 Not everything needs to be ready at once

Combining management systems does not need to be complete at the beginning of the implementation of the OKR system. Often it is impossible because it is very difficult to merge all the details and features by planning alone. Only practice shows everything that needs to be taken into account and changed.

For this reason, the implementation of the OKR model should be done in moderation, for example, according to the following scheduling:
- **Q1:** The leadership has OKRs and each team has the objective of acquainting themselves with the OKR model.
- **Q2:** All teams have OKRs.
- **Q3:** Tracking is active and key results are mainly numerical.
- **Q4:** Retrospectives are in place and OKRs help in guiding the organization's annual clock.

It is common and highly recommended that the organization's first OKRs relate to the implementation of the OKR model itself. This allows you to not only practice the OKR model, but also learn it in a real environment, whilst accomplishing the implementation. Best of all it is action, not just planning.

4.4.2 What management system do we have?

The management system is a collection of all the operating models by which work is done. It can be an extremely accurate process description, documented down in painstaking detail, and audited by an external entity.

Such a management system exists at Labrox, mentioned above, where laboratory equipment vital to human life is being built and even one change in the wrong place at the wrong time can be fatal. Very specific rules and conditions for decision-making, management and processes need to be implemented.

Alternatively, the management system may be a very free-form and shifting collection of different measures: there are Monday meetings, excel files or, for example, a call made by the CEO on Mondays, directing the workforce to the right sites.

Systems aren't right or wrong, they just are. It's only important to be aware of what the current management system of a company is. List and write down the following:
- How is work managed?
- How is it measured?
- How is it planned?
- What is the intake process and how is it processed?
- What meetings are organized and when?
- What, where and why are things reported?

Once the list is complete it will be easier to set out to merge these different mechanisms with the OKR model.

4.4.3 OKRs highlight priorities

In each organization, work is planned and a wide range of measures are taken, all of which results in a pile-up of tasks for employees. These appear as separate, often mutually exclusive priority lists. The management system determines how work requests arrive and what is done with the requests.

Work and priority lists are generated, for example, from the following feeds:
- employee surveys
- risk management
- security forum
- the quality or environmental system
- customer satisfaction survey or customer service
- laws and regulations

The basic premise and purpose of the OKR model is that by looking at it, you can deduce what is important right now. For this reason, the data from all of the forums mentioned above should be taken into account when planning objectives for the following quarter.

The final results must be taken into account at the right level in the organization. For example, top-level targets may not show job assignments that have arrived from the security forum, but for an in-house IT department, they may well make a big difference. When thinking about objectives, each level of the organization should take into account the forums and priority lists relevant to its work.

In addition, it should be remembered that the OKR model only shows what is important right now. That is the change that we want to bring about at the current moment. On top of that, there are normal daily tasks that are managed in job and task management systems and measured by KPI metrics as reported in Chapter Two.

Once the OKR model is in place, employees should be able to unequivocally tell where they should spend their time and energy. They know what's important right now, what the priorities are and what the work they are doing is related to. This brings consistency and security to operational work.

Futurice's tips for the CEO or internal champion

Futurice's OKR internal champion, Viljami Väisänen, gives the CEO or internal champion five tips for starting the OKR journey.

1. Start by being aware of what the current and the aspirational management cultures of your organization are. How does corporate culture differ in different parts of the organization, for example in different countries or different offices? You can refer to this image from Spotify for help:

Spotify's chart of alignment and autonomy (paraphrased by Spotify, 2014).
Based on this, consider the appropriate approach for your organization to the OKR model and its deployment.

At the same time, consider what creates psychological safety and how transparent and equal employees perceive the organization. Successful adoption of the OKR model requires a healthy baseline. However, don't get bogged down with your organization's problems at the beginning. Go and experiment, implementing the OKR model can also serve as a tool to fix the basics.

2. Find a sponsor and make sure that the majority of key players identified are committed. At an organizational level, OKR implementation requires investment and mental resources, especially from managers to make sure that OKRs are made a natural part of the strategy process. It's good to remember that even a single team can benefit from using the OKR model to control its everyday focus. However, the most significant value will emerge when the whole organization is aligned.

3. From the get-go, emphasize the challenge that the implementation of the OKR model aims to address in your organization. Crystallize the answer to the question "why" — from the perspective of the organization as well as the individual — and repeat the message consistently. This will help you, especially with management commitment. Once a challenge is identified, verified, accepted and communicated, individuals find it easier to commit to an experiment that could solve it.

4. Take advantage of multi-channel communication and use good tools instead of your own hacks. In the 1970s, the OKRs of Intel employees were only visible on paper at employees' workstations. It was simple but worked. Today, electronic communication is the default, but the communication may easily be lost in a flood of email and information from more agile communication channels.

Futurice's OKR deployment has been significantly assisted by an investment in a decent OKR tool, BetterWorks. There has also been extensive use of multi-channel communication ranging from OKR canvases hung on walls and face to face gatherings to real-time data on information screens and the intranet. You can never put too much effort into communication. Repeat, repeat and repeat until you hear the audience complain that there is too much communication.

5. Approach it as a journey of continuous learning. The journey won't reach a happy conclusion in a quarter or two. You should draw a map that looks and feels right for you and choose a qualified guide. In addition, when embarking, it is good to be aware that there will be roadblocks that will make many people want to quit.

If successful, the OKR journey will propel your organization towards a more agile, transparent and efficient business. With us, this journey is clearly still in progress and there isn't 100% certainty of success, but so far, the direction has been good — and hey, we keep learning all the time!

Internal champion! Carrying the torch of change can, on bad days, feel like a lonely battle against furiously spinning windmills. The key is to build a network that supports change, igniting the sparks one at a time, conversation by conversation. A good challenge for yourself is to fan the OKR flame so bright that your own role as internal champion becomes invisible. Doing your homework before embarking on this journey will serve you well. The fact that you're reading this book is already a great start.

4.5 Summary and what's next

So far, we have gone through deployment-related phases from project, system and organizational perspectives. This chapter addressed the prerequisites for the implementation of the OKR model, which have a decisive impact on whether or not the deployment is successful. Deployment requires the company to have a strategy as well as enough time for implementing change and for management to be committed and have knowledge of the level of autonomy within the organization. It is also important to know why the OKR model is being implemented in the first place. The answer to this question is the cornerstone of communication for the implementation project.

Of course, deployment also requires certain competence and commitment to change from the organization. The driver of the change is a transformation project team with at least a management representative, staff representative and an internal champion to maintain organizational momentum. We also went through the choice of using software or using another solution.

Finally, we looked at management systems, which the OKR model is an example of. Management systems manage both work and people. Managing people and communicating things is just as important, if not more important, in adopting the OKR model than technical transformation project issues. In the following chapter, we examine expectation management, communication and cultural changes during the implementation of the OKR model.

5 MANAGING CHANGE AND EXPECTATIONS

Strategies are about wanting to bring about change to the status quo. The OKR model is a means to achieve that change. Change always means excitement and worry for employees. It's good news for some and bad news for others. The implementation of the OKR model therefore, requires managing expectations and leading people. There is really only one working tool for that: communication.

As we showed at the beginning of the previous chapter, the implementation process usually goes like this.

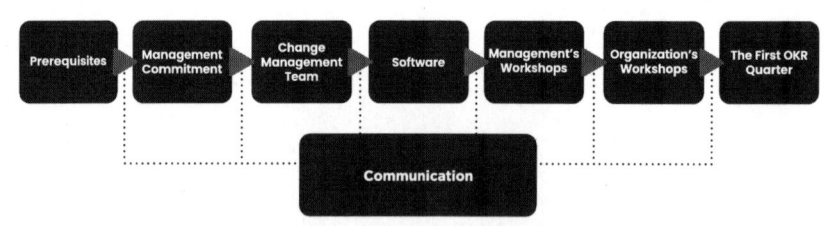

| Prerequisites | Management Commitment | Change Management Team | Software | Management's Workshops | Organization's Workshops | The First OKR Quarter |

Communication

Typical order of progress in implementing the OKR model.

Every single step involves communication: what is being done, why it is being done, who is doing it, in what order and on what schedule. In addition to information, communication should inspire and encourage. Communication also aims at controlling the organization's expectations of change and its consequences. There will be significant communication demands that need to be given attention and resources throughout the implementation.

Generally, transformational projects are good at providing information. Companies are good at letting you know when a project starts or when a new model is put into practice. Organizations often remember to talk about a new project and the people appointed to it. Targets are communicated, software selection is announced, schedules are published and the results of strategic workshops are reported. What may often be forgotten is the communication related to managing expectations and managing people.

Expectation management means that
- different perspectives are taken into account in advance before work is started
- the challenges and steps ahead will be communicated right from the start
- when facing issues, the organization dares to move on despite any inconveniences

The OKR model is simple, but implementing it might be trickier than expected. The implementation phases run into a variety of challenges that need to be solved one way or another. Despite this, there is no need to fear - start boldly. The important thing is to be able to anticipate challenges and communicate them in a correct and timely manner.

This chapter focuses on how to communicate changes in the organization with regards to the OKR model. We have listed the aspects of the implementation of the OKR model that, according to our experience, need careful communication. These are common in many OKR stories and are likely to be so in future OKR implementations as well.

5.1 The objective is to improve business

There is a very good reason for the adoption of the OKR model — and that reason is not the implementation of the OKR model. The OKR model is just an instrument, not an end in itself. Although the reason itself varies from company to company, it always relates to achieving business objectives. Above all, the purpose of the OKR model is organizational change, growth and innovation. The change must eventually be reflected in revenue and earnings.

A large number of transformational projects stumble when the method, model, theory or process itself becomes more important than the goal. That's when the big picture blurs out and things get nitty-gritty. We have seen far too many agile transformations, where agility itself suddenly becomes more important than the client and the outcome. This is especially evident in larger organizations, where people have more time, less customer contact and no vested interest in achieving results.

The debate needs to move away bickering over what kind of key result is "more correct" or "more consistent" with the OKR model, often it is a theory or model that has taken over people's thinking. Whilst it's important to understand how the model works, if a key result or objective describes an outcome that is important to the business *well enough*, it is sufficient. It is more important to get objectives and key results done than arguing about the correctness of each detail.

Therefore, in every planning meeting, it is necessary to reiterate that the goal is not the full implementation of the OKR model itself, but the improvement of the business using the OKR model. When this is crystallized, it's easier to focus on the essentials and avoid over-analyzing when making key results.

Questions to Explore:
- Is it customary for your company to discuss the exact method of implementation of agile or KPI meters?
- Do you have lean police in your organization who condemn some modes of action as either wrong or right from the point of lean?
- Do you get stuck in debates about details and perfect execution, or are you able to look at the big picture and the outcome?

Tips for effective communication:
1. Remember, in all OKR communication and especially at the beginning of the implementation, to share the reason for the implementation. Reiterate it until the organization is saturated with it, it is clear to everyone. After that, remember to stress to teams from time to time why the OKR model has actually been implemented.
2. Add a short section to the beginning of each workshop explaining the reason for implementing OKRs. Remind participants that the task is to improve business, not establish perfect objectives and key results.
3. At the end of the quarter, always communicate how the OKR model has managed to fulfill its intended purpose, or how the journey is progressing towards the desired goal. Share regularly how the OKR model has helped the organization improve business and make work more efficient. Also, highlight what's been learned along the way.

5.2 It's a long road from the initial enthusiasm to the finish line

"Let's do it like Google! The model is simple, so I'm sure it's easy to deploy!" That's where it starts. The initial enthusiasm will get things fired up, but enthusiasm will wane in the face of reality sooner or later. Either the novelty of the new, shiny OKR model wears off — or runs into failures and problems.

Enthusiasm is a wonderful asset, but it needs to be coupled with disciplined work and an unyielding personality. Sometimes these reside in the same individual, often they don't. Therefore, diversity in the organization and especially in the teams, is important. There are enthusiasts and there are finishers, both are needed.

From the get-go, it's good to acknowledge that there will be tough times. For instance:

- The key results have not been updated weekly, so there are surprises at the end of the quarter.
- There are too many objectives and/or too much stretching is required, and none of them have been reached.
- What seemed important at the beginning of the quarter is revealed to be inconsequential at the end of the quarter.
- There is a realization in the middle of the quarter that the key results are actually tasks.
- You realize that your OKR targets are actually KPI metrics.
- You realize that the teams cannot affect the achievement of their objectives through their own work.
- After two quarters, you realize that the objectives thus far are not aligned with the annual objectives.

When this happens, it is necessary to pick yourself up and try again. Even though the initial enthusiasm has subsided by now, the commitment must be maintained. You have to get fired up by remembering what's important, what the goal is, and what you are collectively trying to get done.

It will take a long time to make fundamental changes, and results will be slow. Therefore, it is worth reminding the teams during the early stages of OKR deployment that it takes at least a year to master the model and results only begin to show after multiple quarters. You have to keep going and trust that before long the effects will be visible both in the numbers and in everyday life.

Fortunately, the very first OKR discussions will help to bring focus and clarity to the organization. The satisfaction brought by improved clarity alone gets you through times when updating key results is frustrating.

Questions to Explore:
- Does your organization complete transformational projects?
- What is the ratio of unfinished to finished projects?
- Is your organization good at starting but bad at keeping things going?
- Does the management team have enthusiasts or finishers?

Tips for effective communication:

1. If your organization has so far been good at starting but bad at keeping things going or getting them ready, admit it to the whole organization. Think about how the situation will be corrected for this transformational project, and say it out loud.
2. An even better idea is to ask for correction proposals directly from teams. Organize a workshop and collect ideas from the organization. You can open up a conversation by saying, "We're good at getting excited, but projects tend to stay unfinished and things are not updated in a long-term and disciplined way. What could we as a team do, to make sure this project doesn't lose momentum?"
3. Tell the organization from the start that change is not going to be a straight trajectory towards success. Prepare the organization for incremental change and perseverance. Instead of trying to change things all at once, getting exhausted and giving up, prepare the team for a slow and steady implementation period.
4. Be honest in the quarterly reviews and share both successes and challenges. Compliment people when they come up with good OKR habits that maintain the tracking and implementation of OKRs. Also, make sure that the retrospectives deal with issues related to running the model itself in addition to the results of the objectives.

5.3 Accepting that we are new to this

Almost all the companies we interviewed that are using the OKR model told us that they were still at an "internship" phase. They have accepted that they are practicing the use of the OKR model and learning as they move forward.

Permission to learn by doing is very important since all the nuances of the implementation cannot be planned for.

It is not possible to fully know beforehand what the end result will look like. No matter how much the plan is iterated, even the best plan is a mere guess at the future. Only practical experience will show what influencing factors are hidden in the organization. Each organization is different, so even the details of the implementation are slightly different between organizations. Even an experienced consultant cannot create a neat slideshow with precise instructions. Reality always surprises you.

The main thing, as already noted before, is to start using the OKR model. The model is adapted to the organization one step at a time. One of the cornerstones of the OKR model is that things are done systematically and lessons are learned by doing. This manages the fears and anxiety of change experienced by both management and staff. When the model is not immediately forced into practice, it allows you to build up skills with time and it also helps with often limited resources.

Giving permission to practice by doing is a different effort depending on the organization and culture. Finnish management culture is slowly learning to admit that we are not perfect and we are allowed to practice. Management does not necessarily have all things figured out in detail at the start, but it has a strong belief that the company will be able to solve problems together as they arise.

In Asia for example, the exact opposite is still true. Mistakes are simply not allowed to be made otherwise the person will lose face — and possibly their job. Of course, starting out as imperfect, practicing by doing and allowing failure is impossible in such a culture. It is, therefore, essential to understand the local culture into which the OKR model is being implemented.

Questions to Explore:
- How does the organization typically react when someone fails to complete or succeeds on the first attempt?
- Do we look for culprits, are we collectively ashamed?
- Or are we looking for new perspectives together: what was learned, and how the situation can be improved together?
- Will management representatives tolerate incompleteness?
- Are superheroes and superior individual performances idolized?
- Is talking about lessons learned commonplace?

Tips for effective communication:

1. In OKR communication we should stress that we are not fully ready, but are starting a phased implementation because we want to learn and understand as we progress. This will go on for a long time. There will be mistakes along the way, but we'll fix them and learn from them together.
2. The leadership team needs to act as an example and openly state what lessons have been learned from various failures and lacking performances. A lot of success is also determined by how leadership responds to failures by the rest of the organization.
3. Blaming and defensiveness must be eradicated from communication. In its place, a culture of jointly seeking development ideas and solutions should be fostered. Explore what you want regarding this problem together, how you want this solved, and how you can get the result you want.

5.4 Objectives and key results are difficult in the beginning

Almost all of the OKR stories we collected for this book repeated the same message: The OKR model itself is very easy to understand, but it is surprisingly difficult to implement in practice. But if the model itself is easy to understand, where do the difficulties come from?

The difficulty arises from the fact that in the OKR model one should be able to talk about important issues clearly. Speaking clearly is always harder than speaking vaguely. It requires a clarity of thought from the speaker and a firm understanding of what really is the most important thing, which should then be succinctly communicated to the entire organization.

Another challenge is that objectives and key results force you to make choices and focus on a limited number of things at one time. The selection process is certainly not an easy task, especially in the beginning and especially in organizations that are not used to such a targeted approach.

OKRs bring structure to meeting these challenges. The OKR model only works when the issues that are important to the organization are talked about adequately and clearly. The objectives must be clear to everyone and limited in number for every quarter. This is one of the superpowers of the OKR model:

when the objectives are clear, everyone can aspire towards them — and they are more likely to be achieved.

It is necessary to realize in advance that people will face challenges in explaining the strategic objectives in an understandable way and so in defining the objectives and key results. This challenge may provoke resistance and/or frustration that may appear in the following ways: "This is going to take too much time; can't we just tell everyone what needs to be done."

- "We do not have enough time to do this all the time!"
- "This is useless, a crisis, new strategy, or new project will overrule this one anyway."
- "We need to do all of these at once, this project can't wait three months."
- "This cannot be explained any simpler than it already has!"

When challenges are found, you should celebrate, because finding challenges is important. Without realizing something is a challenge, it is impossible to fix. Once challenges have been identified, they can be resolved and clarity will follow.

If it feels like clarifying strategic objectives or aligning the objectives is cumbersome, then it's worth pausing to think. What could be more important than getting the entire organization to understand what we're heading toward? How else do you make the whole organization's innovations and resources available for the right goal? How else do we ensure that no one inadvertently takes the company in a completely different direction from the chosen direction?

If a company's employees are too busy to set their objectives as current jobs and projects are more critical, it is a sign that choices need to be made. Once those choices are made, things become calmer because not all requests to work on certain issues are urgent or mandatory. Things get done and waste gets eliminated. This is already an important enough reason to stop and take time for the implementation of the OKR model.

If the objectives are not relevant in everyday life and just another thing that needs to be dealt with, then there is no chance of the strategy being implemented in the first place. To reduce the chance of sudden changes in direction we need to reduce organizational uncertainty, contain the flood of conflicting priorities and job queues and instead choose important issues and stick to them.

In terms of expectation management, it is important to remember that with the OKR model, it is perfectly appropriate to say no to work that is not related to OKRs, regardless of where it comes from within the organization. Everyone has the right to point out if something does not relate to the chosen objectives. Refusal may seem foreign at first, but quickly becomes empowering.

Questions to Explore:
- How easily does your organization give up if something is more difficult than management initially thought?
- Does the organization keep trying until it is successful?
- Is there enough time allocated to scoring objectives and key results and to work on them?
- Is everyone willing to accept that the organization systematically cancels projects that are not important at that moment, even if they are considered dear?

Tips for effective communication:

1. Be sure to stress that while the OKR model seems easy, the actual implementation is surprisingly tricky. Encourage people not to give up and remind them that the results will come when we work together. It may be helpful if the OKR experiment is given a clear minimum duration that is long enough. For example, "We'll try the OKR model for a year, and if in a year we don't detect any positive effects, we go back to what we are used to doing".
2. If clarifying and defining objectives causes frustration and resistance, it is important for the management team to take a realistic look at its own work. Maybe the strategy isn't clear after all? Maybe you just do too many different things in the organization? Perhaps the benefits of the model have not been communicated clearly enough?
3. Even before starting the implementation, it is good to take a realistic look at the organization as well. How much work is lined up, how many projects are in progress, and how many ideas are on the table? It helps you understand how challenging setting objectives is going to be. Be sure to tell the entire organization that they now have license to narrow the scope. It's more important to get things ready than start new projects.
4. Use the following picture to remind you that waiting for three months will be faster than doing everything at once.

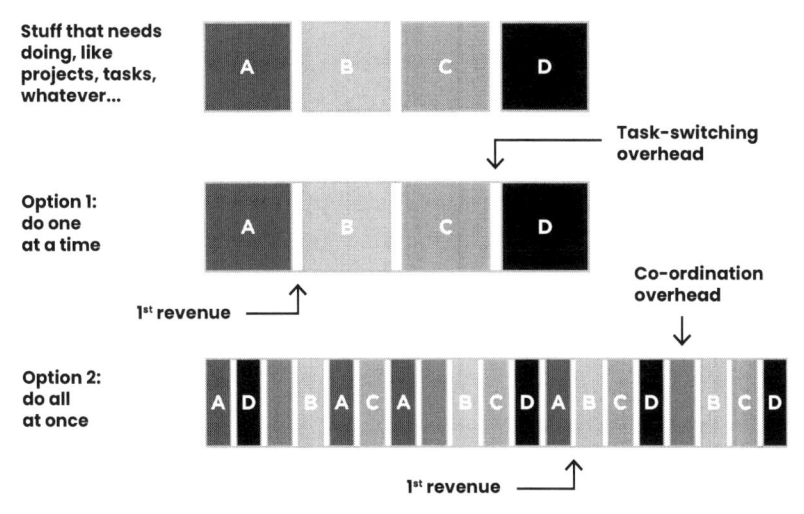

The cost of multiple overlapping projects.

5.5 Continuous improvement requires a culture of learning

The OKR model is not a one-shot solution; it is a model of continuous improvement. This sounds fine on paper, but in practice, it may provoke surprising resistance. Everyone is different, and continued improvement may worry people who:

- tolerate incompleteness poorly and would like to do things perfectly on the first attempt
- fear failure
- fear the loss of power or decision-making rights
- want to stick to tried and true models and habits
- want to plan things into completion before starting

The more people are used to reflecting on their actions and improving them regularly, the smaller the change with the OKR implementation will be. If people are used to toiling the same way day after day, the change is significant and requires empathetic communication.

When the management team or an internal champion presents the OKR model to the organization, it is worth stressing the benefits of its continuously reflective nature. By systematically going through accomplishments and disappointments every quarter, at a minimum it is possible to improve the company, ease the everyday life of the employees, increase the comfort with work, improve customer service, remove the rush and get things ready faster.

You should remember to share that while the OKR model brings patterns and poorly working processes into the light in an organization, OKRs are not a tool for stalking and blaming. The goal is not to point the finger at culprits, but to investigate the operation of the company as a system.

It is also worthwhile for the internal champion or management team to stress that the OKR model does not correct the way an organization operates all at once. Once you make sure that each quarter is even slightly better than the previous one, the organization will become significantly more goal-oriented in just a year.

The model for continuous development of OKRs has the same idea as **William Edwards in Deming's** Quality Circle: Plan—Do—Check—Act.

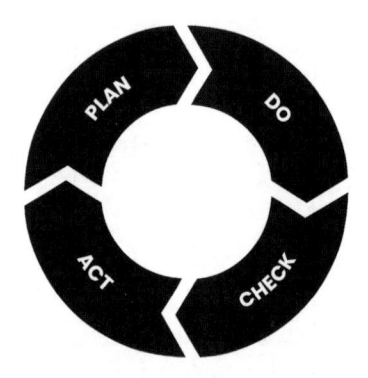

Deming's Quality Circle, modified from the original by Nancy Taguen.

It should be remembered that continuous improvement and ambitious stretch targets require employees to be able to own up to their mistakes and also to fail. Part of the culture of learning is that it is ok to fail as long as the experience has been a learning experience. It is even desirable that errors and weaknesses are brought to light so that lessons can be learned from them and improvements made. So when people bring up their failures, mistakes and grievances with the system we need to thank them and not admonish them.

Stretch, failures and continuous improvement might unexpectedly be the hardest of all for leaders. Often, they can be "meet the numbers" people who produce the desired figures for the organization. For them, failure has in the past been considered a horrible sin. With OKRs, this is completely different as stretch goals are rooted in being unreachable. If all are achieved, there was not enough stretch in the objectives. This may require a significant mind shift for some leaders within an organization.

Questions to Explore:
- Are your OKRs always "complete" at the beginning of each quarter, or are they just the best effort at that moment with the current understanding of things?
- Are mistakes, lessons, trial and error talked about openly in the company, or is everything swept quietly under the rug as if nothing happened?
- Are people encouraged to experiment?
- Has reflection been commonplace, or is this a whole new operating model for the company?

Tips for effective communication:
1. Communicate that the OKR model involves systematic and continuous improvement. The process of making a change involves a continuous and honest retrospective process. Emphasize that the management team is very interested in the outcome of the retrospectives as snapshots of the current state and that they help in developing a stronger company.
2. Emphasize that no one is pointing fingers, nor looking for perpetrators to punish. The more we as a company can evolve and learn, the better it is for everyone. The goal of the OKR model is to make the organization more flexible and adaptable. It can only be done through experimentation and learning. Conjecture and over-planning will only result in half-baked efforts.
3. Remind the organization that OKRs are sequential sprints done sustainably. It is not the intention to work the organization to death but to build strength and improve performance. The intention is that we start a life-long journey together — not just survive through to the next quarter or to the end of the year.

5.6 Radical transparency is the default

The transparency of the OKR model might be a tough spot for some of the company's employees. It's easy to think that only those with something to hide are against transparency. However, people are different, especially in what they would like to keep to themselves. Even if their work is flawless, some still prefer to remain invisible and inconspicuous.

Transparency is a crucial part of the OKR model as it allows the company to align what it does and *see*, in concrete terms and how the work of different departments and teams affects the work of others. The objectives of all teams are public and so alignment can be done at all levels, not just from the top down. Aimlessness, vagueness and ambiguity disappear and the importance of the work is strengthened when everyone understands their role in the grand plan as well as the strategic objective of the company.

It is only possible to achieve this by making all objectives visible to everyone. This transparency can even be radically different from the past mode of operation, where decisions and projects may have been made behind closed doors. The management team, in particular, may have gotten used to directing the action invisibly, from behind closed doors. By implementing the OKR model, the doors are opened and the objectives are revealed to everyone.

From a communication perspective, the transparency of objectives may initially cause discomfort. Leadership plays a big role in setting an example by choosing how they inform their objectives and by emphasizing transparency. It should also be acknowledged that when using the OKR model, people can focus on individual performance data, even though OKRs are not a system for measuring individual performance.

It is good to stress that the transparency of the OKR model is not meant to enable snooping or stalking but to help everyone see what is important and therefore address any tendency in the culture for gossip, hearsay and blaming.

Questions to Explore:
- Do you dare to write objectives openly for everyone to see, for example on an intranet? - If this is not the case, what is stopping you?
- Do people tend to point out other people's mistakes or flaws?
- Do people take pleasure in the failures of others?

Tips for effective communication:

1. Start by making sure that all leaders and managers accept transparency and are willing to communicate their objectives openly. Their example is very important in getting transparency accepted by the organization.

2. Communicate that everyone's objectives are visible so that anyone can see what matters to others and help in reaching common objectives. Transparency is the basis for dialogue and for challenging and developing the organization.
3. Stress that no one is monitored and teams will not be ranked in any way based on how they achieve their objectives.

5.7 Change accelerates over time

We are used to making detailed long-term objectives in the form of annual budgets and five-year-plans. In the OKR model, the long term is represented by the vision and annual objectives are the long term objectives.

It is a cliché to say that today the world changes too quickly for precise annual plans. One acronym that describes the modern world is VUCA (*volatility, uncertainty, complexity,* and *ambiguity*), which describes how fast and uncontrollably things change. The OKR model is particularly well suited to combat the growing chaos.

The OKR model sets objectives and key results for the coming quarter only — not the quarter that follows it. Thoughts and assumptions about the following quarters may exist, but they are not written into the annual plan. Assumptions and thoughts are considered only when planning for the next quarter begins.

Since planning is always limited to a period of three months, the OKR model makes it possible to react quickly to changes in competitors, infectious diseases, the global economy, or anything else. Sometimes a quarter isn't enough though. In Section *7.8 Changing OKRs in a crisis situation*, we present a scenario where the circumstances change radically in the middle of the quarter and an immediate reaction is needed. In general, it is possible to maintain the cadence of quarterly planning, which is already very agile compared to many other organizations not using OKRs.

With quarterly planning, the company's strategic agility and ability to change direction will increase significantly, as the company is not tied to a year-long, or even longer, plan. With a quarterly cycle, even a big company can change direction just as quickly as a startup. Startups on the other hand, when they commit to objectives for an entire quarter have a better focus on what happens.

If a company has been comfortable with building detailed plans, it can be difficult to give that up. Planning brings a false sense of security and control. In reality, we cannot control what the future holds, and the best way to survive in a VUCA world is to improve the speed of change and reduce the need for control.

Questions to Explore:
- Is your organization able to accept the uncertainty that follows from setting targets for the year, but only planning for only the next three months?
- Is it acceptable that the sense of control diminishes when plans are not as detailed? Is your organization ready to respond to change at a quarterly level?
- Are you able to focus on what is important without losing sight of the big picture right now?

Tips for effective communication:
1. Prepare for feelings of uncertainty by sharing the fact that because you can't accurately anticipate what's to come, creating detailed plans is most often a waste of time. Emphasize that by using less effort on long-term planning, you can focus better on current challenges, which enhances competitiveness and gives more opportunities for positive change.
2. It is good to emphasize that you are committing to trialing the OKR model for a set amount of time. It gives people peace of mind if they know when testing that if the model is not a perfect fit for their own or the organization's needs, it can be dropped. Plan lovers in particular, need tangible experiences with the benefits of a shorter planning cycle to be able to let go of their old ways.
3. If you're managing a startup that's used to changing plans quickly, be sure to emphasize that there's no use in starting things unless you also get those things done. After three months of focusing on just five objectives, results will begin to show. It's important to be agile, but the line between agility and manic panic is razor-thin. The OKR model helps you to stay agile but also get things done.

5.8 Soon the teams will gain more autonomy

Team autonomy refers to the ability of teams to make their own interpretations and decisions based on the environment. Things that require decision-making may include the execution of a strategy, how customers are served, or the use of the premises. These types of situation are encountered every day and here are some ones:
- Do new laptops need to be requested from management, or through the ticketing system from the HR department, or can the necessary tools be bought out of pocket and the invoice expensed?
- Can you agree on non-standard terms of delivery with the customer, or do you have to seek permission from the CEO?
- Can you switch the brand of a product or component that is ordered or does the decision have to be pushed through the approval process?
- Can a new marketing campaign be launched, or do we have to wait for approval from the management team?
- Can you organize a Christmas party for your team?

The level of autonomy of a mature, long-standing team can be very high: its members know the customs and principles of the company and the industry, and their actions and judgment are trusted. On the other hand, a fledgling team early in their career usually needs a lot of advice and instruction to learn the necessary skills. With each step, they evolve into an increasingly independent unit. An organization may have teams operating at very different levels of autonomy.

Autonomous decision-making is particularly important when OKRs are being planned. How freely are teams allowed to determine their own objectives? As we discussed in section 3.4.2 *Interpreting the objectives in the team*, objectives may be handed to the team in extreme situations. In the other extreme, teams have complete freedom to suggest what they are going to do, with leadership only observing and approving. There are a lot of alternatives between the two extremes.

Since different teams are at different levels of maturity, their level of autonomy can also be different. The leadership team needs to decide what levels of autonomy each team can have and communicate the result on a per-team basis. It is also good to state that autonomy will increase as the team takes more responsibility and carries out its duties without external monitoring. This encourages teams to grow their skills.

Questions to Explore:
- Has there been talk of autonomy in your organization?
- Are there different processes within your organization, or does everyone do things the same way?
- Do team lineups change, or are they static?
- How do you increase the level of autonomy for individuals, and where are the limits?

Tips for effective communication:

1. It is worth going through what team autonomy means on an organizational level. Transparency on the different levels of autonomy within teams and the rationale behind it help teams understand why some are allowed to make decisions more independently and others less so. We also recommend giving teams more responsibility than they have been given in the past — but also staying available for questions and discussing doubts.
2. The OKR model is a model that encourages autonomy and is built on the assumption that teams and employees are capable of managing objectives for themselves and managing their affairs. It is important for the leadership team to encourage teams to create proposals for their objectives to see how well teams can analyze the annual objectives and turn them into quarterly objectives.
3. To reap significant benefits from the OKR model, increasing the level of autonomy is worthwhile. This also requires responsible action from everyone, both within the leadership team and without. As communication between teams and the leadership team increases, it quickly becomes apparent how different teams see the big picture and how much responsibility they want to take for their work.

5.9 Summary and what's next

In this chapter, we have looked at some of the issues that arise in a typical OKR implementation and in which considered communication is particularly important. Essential to OKR communication is making things simple enough and using plain language. When you communicate with an organization, you are communicating with everyone.

Things and choices that should be communicated:
- The implementation of the OKR model will not be completed at once and every step forwards is an improvement.
- Challenges will appear, but you shouldn't worry about them. Problems will be solved together.
- We don't have to be perfect immediately, we are learning by doing.
- The most important thing is to learn from mistakes and be honest in your scoring and evaluations.
- No one will be singled out; we will make improvements together.
- The OKR model brings good changes that will make us better.

We cannot stress enough the importance of communication. Whilst implementation of the OKR model may well fail because of too little communication, we have never heard of a case where it has failed because of too much communication. So, rather communicate too much than too little.

Keep in mind that different people absorb knowledge best in different formats. Share information through speech, text, and video. Use all available communication channels. Be persistent.

The following chapter also relates to communication as we present the typical pitfalls of the implementation project. Many of them can be avoided and fixed through communication. It's good to know the pitfalls so you know how to avoid them — but also to identify them when you are in one. You always get up from them, as long as you're willing to admit mistakes were made and you are willing to correct them.

It is also important to understand common pitfalls as they are seldom talked about. It's easy to imagine you being alone with your problem and the only one who has experienced it. In reality, the pit has been visited by a surprising number of organizations on the way to successful implementation. Support is not only available by reading the next chapter, but also from other organizations sharing the same journey.

6 CROSSING THE VALLEY OF DEATH

Everyone has sometimes experienced how, after initial enthusiasm, a full stop occurs in a project. What was done up until a week ago with enthusiasm will either turn sluggish or cease altogether. OKRs are no exception in this regard.

We have witnessed several OKR deployment projects where the brisk pace at the start fades, or a few months into a project, it is discovered that no progress has been made. We call this the mid-project valley of death. Since both the OKR model and its implementation are company-specific, each transformation project is different and so the valley of death is also a little different.

Often the valley of death is brought on by a familiar change management challenge. These challenges are assembled and aptly described in the well-known model called *Leading and Managing Complex Change*.

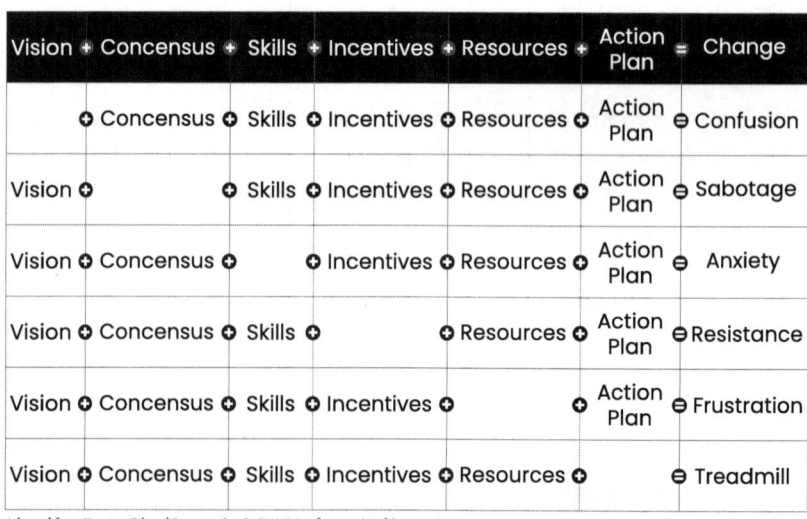

Vision +	Concensus +	Skills +	Incentives +	Resources +	Action Plan	= Change
	✚ Concensus ✚	Skills ✚	Incentives ✚	Resources ✚	Action Plan	⊖ Confusion
Vision ✚		✚ Skills ✚	Incentives ✚	Resources ✚	Action Plan	⊖ Sabotage
Vision ✚	Concensus ✚		✚ Incentives ✚	Resources ✚	Action Plan	⊖ Anxiety
Vision ✚	Concensus ✚	Skills ✚		✚ Resources ✚	Action Plan	⊖ Resistance
Vision ✚	Concensus ✚	Skills ✚	Incentives ✚		✚ Action Plan	⊖ Frustration
Vision ✚	Concensus ✚	Skills ✚	Incentives ✚	Resources ✚		⊖ Treadmill

Adapted from Knoster, T (1991) Presentation in TASH Conference, Washington, D.C.
Adapted by Knoster from Enterprise Group, Ltd.

The management model of complex change, adapted from the Lippitt-Knoster model.

To the best of our understanding, the model was created in 1987 by **Mary Lippitt**. At the time, the model had five components: vision, skills, incentives, resources and action plan. In 1991, Timothy Knoster added a sixth component, consensus (or buy-in) to the model.

According to the Lippitt-Knoster model, successful transformation consists of six components. The members of the organization must first understand what the common **vision** is: where we are going and why. After that, employees need to have a **consensus** on whether the direction is right and a belief that the direction is important.

To achieve the outcome, the right **skills** are needed. Everyone must also see what the **incentives** for change are. In other words, what the benefits of change are for both the individual and the organization. For the change to be successful, adequate **resources** need to be allocated, with time being the most common resource. The success is ultimately assured by a clear **action plan.**

The implementation of the OKR system is a perfect example of a transformational project, to which the Lippitt-Knoster model applies. Most often, challenges in implementing the OKR model can be identified as belonging to one of these six components of change management. We, therefore, go through the potential valleys of death in this chapter through different scenarios of the Lippitt-Knoster model. We also examine how they can be avoided and how to move forward from them.

6.1 Confusion occurs when there is no direction

| ⊕ Concensus | ⊕ Skills | ⊕ Incentives | ⊕ Resources | ⊕ Action Plan | ⊖ Confusion |

Lack of direction causes confusion.

In general, the lack of direction is related to the lack of vision. Confusion results if employees do not know where the organization is going and why. In this scenario, there is no consensus on what the common future is, where the finish line is or what *good* looks like.

When managing change, lack of vision is linked to not understanding why it is relevant to make a change. In adopting the OKR model, a common direction will be lacking unless the reasons behind implementing OKRs are communicated early and often enough. Confusion is especially common when it is not clear to people what the organization is trying to achieve by implementing the OKR model.

This happens quite easily if leadership, who themselves understand the value of the OKR model, enthusiastically apply it to the organization but forget about change management. Sometimes we forget to communicate things we find self-evident.

How do you detect confusion?

A common feature for all death valleys is that things are not moving forward. This is also the case with confusion. When people in an organization are confused, you do not progress because people don't understand what action to take. If progress does not happen or it grinds to a halt, it is good to start looking for reasons.

Another symptom of confusion is language. It can be seen in the following types of word choices: "What's this now?", "Where did this come from?", "What good are these?", "Yet another new system/priority list.", "What are they trying to achieve with this?", "What's the point of this?"

Confusion can also be felt in the atmosphere: the mood is subdued, attitudes are reluctant, and facial expressions are quizzical. Things get done when prompted — but people do not take pleasure in working, brainstorming, or innovating.

If there is a suspicion that employees might be confused, you get to the bottom by asking employees good questions. An anonymous poll or one-on-one discussions with people will quickly reveal whether the value of the OKR model is understood and the direction of change is clear.

Avoid closed questions where people can guess the 'correct' answer, or can be answered with a yes or no for example, "Is implementing the OKR model important to the success of our company?" Instead, a better open question is: "How or why is implementing the OKR model important to the success of our company?"

How can confusion be avoided?

If the project has not yet been started, confusion can be avoided with communication. In Section 4.1.2 *Why is the OKR model implemented?* We noted that the most important thing to communicate accurately and clearly is why OKRs are being implemented. The importance of communication grows the larger the organization is and the greater the change will be.

In all OKR communication, you should always emphasize the following:
- Why is the OKR system being implemented and what is the objective?
- What kind of cultural change is desired, and why?
- What can OKRs achieve?
- Why is the implementation of OKRs a good thing for all members of the organization?

As **Samuel Johnson,** a British 18th century writer, aptly said, "People need to be reminded more often than they need to be instructed." After a manager thinks they have spoken about a common direction and future until everyone is fed up, only then does the message begin to take hold. Communicating change in enthusiastic and clear language is paramount to eliminating confusion and for change to begin at every level of the organization.

Eventually, the vision becomes clearer through working together and seeing results. This is where the internal champion of the OKR project shines. The OKR model will begin to become tangible objectives and key results in inspiring workshops organized by the internal champion. So, it pays to think carefully when selecting your internal champion.

How do you survive confusion?

If the project is already underway and it is discovered that things are not moving forward and confusion has paralyzed people, it is time to return to the inspiring speeches from earlier on in the project; assemble everyone and address issues directly. Confusion can be alleviated by actively clarifying again and again, what the end goal is.

It is particularly useful to focus on "what good looks like," that is, what the future will look like. It's good to reflect on what good OKRs will bring and how OKRs help the organization move together towards that future. Discuss what good looks like through the eyes of a customer, employee, organization and the world.

It is not worthwhile to fear confusion either since all new things seem confusing at first. That is why we have stressed in previous chapters that excessive planning and the pursuit of perfection is futile: it is important to just get going. Confusion eases with experience as things become clear when seen in practice.

6.2 Lack of common understanding leads to sabotage

Vision ⊕		⊕ Skills	⊕ Incentives	⊕ Resources	⊕ Action Plan	⊖ Sabotage

Lack of consensus causes sabotage.

The first potential death valley is caused by a lack of vision and the resulting confusion. Another potential death valley arises if people don't believe in the chosen direction. At worst, some of the organization's employees may even actively hamper or slow the adoption of the OKR model.

Timothy Knoster added this phenomenon to Mary Lippitt's model and described the lack of consensus as sabotage. Essential to the Knoster amendment is that consensus means not only a mere passive understanding of change but also a belief in the chosen direction, an active acceptance of it.

Lack of acceptance comes from employees not agreeing with the chosen goal. Some may feel that the direction is simply not good. Some resist the new direction because they fear giving up old ways, some live in a nostalgic fantasy where the current state is the best. Others dislike the direction because the proposal did not come from them. When a person does not actively accept a direction, the result is **subversion**.

An actively subversive individual
- questions the objective through witty questions and heckling,
- hampers progress by hiding their work,
- actively or passively resists the progress of the project,
- tries to convince others to join them in resisting the change,
- hides necessary information,
- is leading the organization in a diametrically opposite direction to what was agreed upon together.

Often these situations originate from the fact that people have not been allowed to participate sufficiently in setting a direction, they have not been listened to, they have not had the opportunity to share their opinions and views and have not been included in the development stages of the vision. A direction solely originating from the leadership team often provokes opposition, even if it has been communicated clearly.

How to recognize subversion?
Passive-aggressive behavior is the most difficult to identify of counter-reac-

tions, as it often happens behind the backs of leaders. Where confusion may be talked about openly, lack of consensus is the subject of water cooler conversations.

It is not uncommon for managers when in the presence of leadership, to agree and be involved in change. But the following week, the same managers will tell their employees a completely different story: "This is just another fancy initiative. Just report something to keep them happy, but no need to put too much effort into it."

One manifestation of this is the "meeting after the meeting" mentioned in **Brené Brown's** book *Dare to Lead*. Brown describes how, after a meeting, back-channeling begins in the hallways behind the manager's back. Things that should have been said in the meeting are now hidden gossip.

Subversion can be best observed by chatting with different people from every level of the organization. If middle management actively tries to hamper the OKR project with their employees, the situation may be revealed by chatting with those employees. Sometimes the lack of consensus is also reflected in dismissive comments, eye-rolling and sighing during meetings and workshops.

How can subversion be avoided?

The earlier people can influence and the more they can influence change, the deeper the consensus will be. Allowing people to share their ideas and concerns shows that their opinions are heard.

Patrick Lencioni's book *The Five Dysfunctions of a Team* states that in principle, people accept a decision contrary to their own view, as long as they have been able to tell them they disagree. People should feel that they have been heard and understood, even if the decision is not what they wanted.

There may be fear that change will bring visibility to issues that used to be safely hidden. The transparency of the OKR system can be daunting if someone has previously been able to present things as being better organized and themselves as performing better than they actually have. The requirement for transparency may also cause concern within the leadership team.

It is possible to prevent the problem by emphasizing from the beginning that there is no need to be afraid of failure - not reaching objectives isn't a punishable offense. The only thing you have to worry about is that you learn from these failures. Even if it seems obvious, it may be necessary to state aloud more than once that the purpose of implementing the OKR system is not to fire those who do not reach their objectives.

The OKR model raises the bar for the entire organization; it always exposes flaws, grievances and processes that do not work — and that's perfectly acceptable. Transparency must bring the real situation to light in the organization. On this basis, decisions can be made and improved. The intent is not to show defects in people, but in methods and processes — and how to improve things together.

How do you get rid of subversion?

As transparency increases, the actions of an individual who is slowing or hampering progression tend to be revealed. For example, if someone tries to continue to advance their own goals by having other objectives and projects that are not in the OKR system, they usually come to light. As the setting, progress and results of objectives are discussed together regularly, it becomes increasingly difficult to hide work and dodge OKRs.

Attempts to prevent the adoption of the OKR itself can be curbed by setting the implementation of the OKRs as the first OKR. We almost always recommend this. The implementation of the OKR model should be a common task for the whole organization, so it is a logical first OKR objective. If a person tries to prevent or slow the progress of OKR implementation, they end up preventing themselves from reaching their own objectives as well. This usually becomes visible immediately after the first quarter.

Harmful behavior needs to be tackled without prejudice. There are plenty of organizations that allow individuals their tantrums and other unacceptable behavior under the guise of someone "being a tough sales cannon" or "if this coder leaves, then all systems will crash". Enabling unacceptable behavior is an unsustainable solution in the long run since such exceptional cases will corrupt the culture and morale of the rest of the organization. A prerequisite for the success of the OKR model is disciplined action that applies to everyone.

6.3 Anxiety is a result of a lack of skills

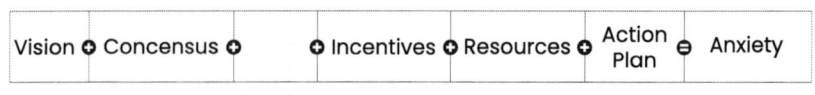

Vision ⊕ Concensus ⊕	⊕ Incentives ⊕ Resources ⊕	Action Plan	⊖ Anxiety

When skills are lacking, it causes anxiety.

The third type of problem in change management arises in a situation where workers lack the necessary and sufficient skills to achieve the objective. The fear that your skills are not enough to deal with the new situation causes stress and anxiety in people.

The implementation of the OKR model may require competence from the staff that has either not been needed at all in the past or has been utilized very differently. You should, for instance, know how to write inspirational objectives and measurable key results. The requirement for measurability is not exactly an easy thing to put into practice. In addition, everyone should be able to plan work both at a strategic level and in three-month implementation cycles.

For teams, setting their own objectives can be very difficult at first — especially if objectives have previously been dictated top-down. In the worst-case scenario, they have been told how to implement those objectives and how to do the job in practice; leaving teams with very little decision power and opportunities for independent action.

There is also a significant increase in demand from leaders and a new structure is needed for management practices. If there's been a lightweight weekly meeting with a bit of chatting in the past and things have somewhat progressed - OKRs bring quite a change. The key results set in the OKR model must be followed up on and tracking must be a disciplined practice.

In addition, managers need interaction skills to:
- connect with team members and detect when people need help
- encourage and inspire change
- dare to admit when they have not succeeded in something

The role of the leader may change more or less, depending on the baseline. OKRs bring more transparency and autonomy for everyone. If the manager has been used to dictating, the change is rather drastic.

All these new situations and requirements may create a feeling that your own skills are not enough. A lot of things are taken over in the OKR model at once and it might seem insurmountable at first. That's when anxiety wants to take over.

How to identify anxiety?

Anxiety is related to experiencing insecurity. A sense of security fades once an employee starts feeling that they do not know how they will be able to carry out what is expected of him. If anxiety is not detected, discussed and treated; a wide range of reactions and phenomena may follow.

In an OKR project anxiety can appear for example, as avoidance of tasks when someone is afraid to take action. Constant excuses and even sick leave can also be the result of latent anxiety. On the other hand, anxiety can also appear as bravado and apparent achievement. The right things however, still remain undone. A person putting on a brave face may not seem anxious but is nevertheless masking the uncertainty and turmoil that lies beneath the surface.

Anxiety is a psychological phenomenon with symptoms that vary by person. Therefore, it can be difficult to identify right away, especially if the reaction of someone differs significantly from the observer's reaction. The classic trinity of reactions is *flight, fight, freeze.*

In the book, *Radical Collaboration: Five Essential Skills to Overcome Defensiveness and Build Successful Relationships* by James W. Tamm and Ronald J. Luyet, a total of 50 different signs for concluding a person is defensive are presented. These include:
- disappearance of a sense of humor
- desire to have the "last word" in the debate
- denial
- sarcasm
- blaming
- black and white thinking
- addiction
- overt kindness
- rapid heartbeat or breathing

In language, when a person is capable of acknowledging their anxiety, it appears in phrases such as: "I don't know how to do this.", "I'm scared, I'm worried.", "No one has told me how to do this.", "I don't know how." and "This seems difficult, horrible and messy."

When they do not acknowledge their anxiety the language an be very different, appearing in phrases like, "What's the point of this?", and "Why do we have to change now when what we do has always worked before?"

One typical manifestation of anxiety in OKR implementation projects is the attempt to be perfect immediately - which slows down the adoption. It leads to overthinking and months spent on planning, perfecting and discussions. In such situations, unreasonable amounts of energy are used on worrying about what will happen if everything doesn't go according to plan. These are all signs of anxiety when starting to use the OKR model.

How can anxiety be avoided?
To avoid anxiety, we must communicate from the beginning that the OKR implementation is going according to plan, even when plans fail. Each failure

yields information crucial to the organization. Improvements have to start somewhere and getting started is a thousand times more important than being perfect.

From the start, there should be an emphasis on learning: that this is something we are learning together. The main thing is to start doing. The outcome is good enough when we are practicing by doing it together. This eliminates the fear that competence is not at the required level because according to the plan, everyone starts at the current level of knowledge.

Of course, theory and learning materials need to be provided and enough people in the organization should know the OKR model well. These internal champions train managers who in turn, know how to answer questions when they arise. The manager practices by doing it with someone who knows the model too.

It is also good to occasionally view the implementation and progression of the OKR model impartially. A regular retrospective with the internal champion is a great tool for this.

How to deal with anxiety?

If anxiety is discovered in the middle of a project, the situation should be tackled gently. Treat the origin of the anxiety - bring up the situation with the individual, without judgment and discuss the skills they feel are lacking.T. It's good for a manager to learn to tell at what stage they're at with their own learning and what they have had to practice so that others feel able to talk to them about their own feelings of incompleteness.

Opportunities to identify skill gaps and anxiety happen more easily once OKRs become part of weeklies and performance reviews and OKR development is openly talked about together. It is vitally important for the entire team to see identified issues as opportunities to grow and not as failures.

When an employee frets over whether an objective or key result is inspiring enough, accurately measurable, perfectly stated and perfectly aligned; the manager's job is to encourage experimentation. Therefore, it is worthwhile to set up the actual first OKR model as part of the first OKRs. In this case, the objectives are valid even if the work would not be perfect.

You can also always refer to **Bruce Lee** and kung-fu. The difference between a white belt and a black belt is that the black belt has failed more times than the white belt has attempted. We only grow to have less spectacular failures. We will never reach perfection, nor should it be our objective.

6.4 Resistance will grow if there are no rewards

Vision ⊕ Concensus ⊕ Skills ⊕	⊕ Resources ⊕	Action Plan	⊖ Resistance

Missing incentives cause resistance.

At times, an exhilarating vision can take you far. Simon Sinek's book, *Start with Why*, tells us that a simple, inspiring "why?" can move mountains. The bigger an organization gets, the more likely it is to have people in the mix for whom an inspiring goal is not sufficient in itself. Everyone is, in principle, the protagonist of their own story, and unless the benefits of the OKR model are clear to the individual, getting motivated by the implementation of the model is difficult. If incentives are missing, resistance may start to emerge from within the organization.

Resistance may arise for the same reasons as sabotage. If a person is just told to use the OKR model, they will probably oppose it. If the reasons for change are not inspiring enough, or it is solely dictated from above, an essential component is missing.

This may happen if the communication regarding the OKR model has been painted with too broad strokes that do not tangibly relate to everyday life in the organization. An inspiring vision will sustain a person for a while through difficulties, but not endlessly. It is important to remind individuals how they will benefit from the OKR model in their daily lives. An incentive, i.e. a demonstration of benefits, is needed.

One problematic aspect of the implementation of the OKR model is that it should not be tied to bonus schemes, as further discussed in section 7.4 *Rewards and OKRs*. Since OKRs should never be tied to financial bonuses, they lack the most typical incentive - money. The importance of communicating everyday benefits therefore, is even more important.

How to detect resistance?

Resistance can be easily identified when you hear phrases such as: "I do not see what good this does.", "This does not apply to me, this does not benefit me.", "This is not in my targets." I have more important things to do.", "What's in it for me?" or "Same pay, more work."

Sometimes resistance is difficult to spot, as the arrival of "yet another system or list of priorities" may only cause quiet muttering. If a person is goal-oriented and performance-oriented, they are likely to implement these requirements too — and complain and suffer while they do so.

Resistance, like confusion, can be best observed by asking about it directly. Do not ask, "Do you see that OKRs are beneficial to you?", as it is easy to answer in the affirmative, even if the person answering would have no clue. Most often, ego or fear of losing face prevents a person from admitting that they don't understand enough to be able to act in line with expectations.

Instead, use an open question: "How do OKRs benefit you in your work?". You can easily tell from the answer how well the benefits of the OKR system are understood and absorbed. If their answer is ambiguous it gives you the opportunity to open the conversation further and influence how they feel about OKRs.

How can you avoid resistance?

The key to a successful OKR implementation and avoiding opposition is communicating incentives. From the outset, it is important to stress what the general benefits of OKRs are for both the individual and the organization as a whole. OKRs help you achieve the following:

- Individuals get more freedom to determine their objectives and decide how they intend to implement them.
- More learning opportunities are discovered for the organization as a whole.
- Everybody gets an appropriate amount of added responsibility for their own work.
- Fewer projects are going on when you focus on just a few important issues.
- It is easier to prioritize work when it is clear to everyone what's most important right now.
- Work becomes transparent, and people can see what the value of their work is in relation to the objectives and vision of the organization.
- It is clear to everyone what the objective is and whether it is being reached.
- Permission to try new things and reach further because failing to reach objectives is not punished.

As we have mentioned before, it is wise to make understanding the OKR model as the first objective. Once that goal is reached, it is instantly rewarding. Often a big incentive for people with the OKR model is that they have permission to say *no* to projects and work that are not in the objectives of the current quarter.

This clarity and focus most often brings a significant sense of relief.

How do you deal with resistance?

It is important to both acknowledge and address any behavior which is contrary toT the common line, tasks and policies. Once the reasons for the behavior are understood they are able to be addressed. This requires leaders to be able to to bring things up succinctly with individuals and if necessary be able to have uncomfortable conversations. This applies equally if an individual is not able to modify their approach in accordance with the OKR model.

Ben Horowitz's book *What You Do is Who You Are — How to Create Your Business Culture* states that the culture of the organization is formed by the behavior and acts that people are allowed to carry out: "There's a saying in the military that if you see something below standard and do nothing, you have set a new standard. This is true of culture as well — if you see something inappropriate and ignore it, you have created a new culture."

Culture is formed through actions and especially the actions and behavior we are prepared to tolerate, rather than through words. It is woefully typical of organizations to tolerate a few misbehaving individuals because they get results. This is very short-sighted, as it sends a clear message to the whole organization: you can break the rules and do whatever you want as long as you get results.

Allowing exceptions devalues the currency of the accepted and more widely demonstrated behaviors . Therefore, during the implementation of the OKR model, there is an obligation to intervene and address cases of sabotage and resistance. It is important everyone understands the importance of their own and others' behavior and their role in contributing to a successful OKR implementation.

Instead of blaming people, it is extremely important to try to understand which emotions, fears and thought patterns lie behind the unacceptable behavior. Encountering a person as a whole and as a human being is the only way to get them to openly share the reasons for their behavior. Intervention must be gentle but demanding.

Ultimately, the very last resort in dealing with resistance or sabotage is to let the individual seek new opportunities outside of the company. Unacceptable and even harmful activity is often tolerated for too long. This is very expensive for the organization, and the damage done may continue to be noticed over a long period of time after the person leaves. No individual is worth ruining the whole company culture.

6.5 Frustration as a result of a lack of resources

| Vision ⊕ Concensus ⊕ Skills ⊕ Incentives ⊕ | ⊕ Action Plan | ⊖ Frustration |

Lacking resources causes frustration.

The most typical death valley is lack of resources, especially time. It's the most frustrating of death valleys for employees. It's frustrating if you see the benefit of the change for your work and that of others, as well as for the functioning of the organization as a whole, but it takes so many resources and time that you are unable to do it. *"I'd like to, but I don't have any damn time!"*

You end up in a situation where you already expect people to do too many things at the same time, and then you're adding a little more on top. This is what happens when everything is seen as a priority and everything should be ready right away. In this situation, it is difficult to see what should be abandoned and it is also not understood how much waste and extra work is created simply by having more than one project at a time.

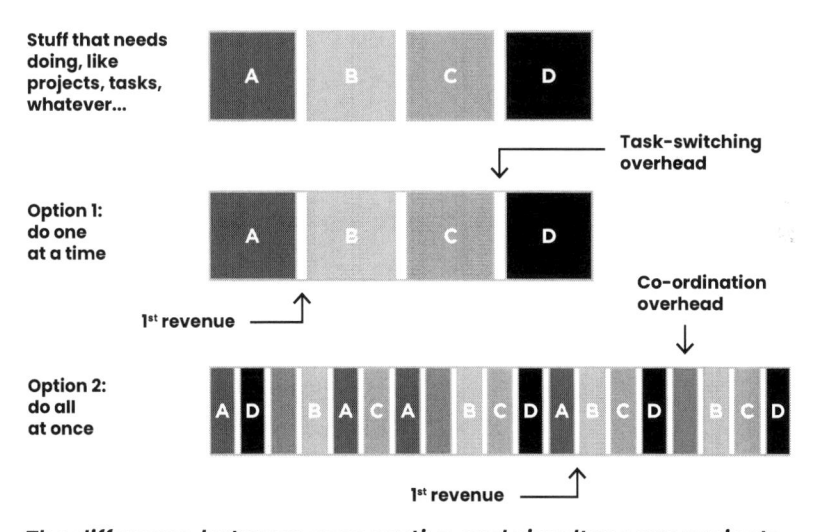

The difference between consecutive and simultaneous projects.

When the gray bars (coordination between different projects, status meetings, and communication) and white task switching bars are removed, all time and functional waste becomes visible.

Option 1:
do one
at a time   Waste!

Option 2:
do all
at once   Waste!

The waste generated by different project management models.

Doing many things at once is both slow, eats up a lot of people's mental capacity and is a huge waste of resources.

If the situation in the beginning is that there is too much to do and too few resources, the implementation of the OKR model may halt quickly. On the other hand, implementing the OKR model would be just the right medicine for this ailment, as long as the process is started. OKRs help us prioritize and focus. Their purpose is to reduce work in progress, not increase it.

CASE: Incorrect use of the OKR model increases the amount of chaos

The purpose of the OKR model is to clarify what is important, and reduce ambiguity when prioritizing work. But we know a few stories where the opposite has happened.

One Finnish company decided to implement the OKR model towards the end of 2018. The decision to implement the OKR model was announced to the personnel and it was also announced that all were to have the first objectives and key results defined for 2019 before the Christmas holidays.

Five objectives were defined at the enterprise level and each had five key results. Under that, five objectives and key results were also defined for each team. In addition to this, everyone had to plan personal objectives and key results. The leadership team also required that everyone had to monitor the company, team and their personal objectives - meaning one person had 15 objectives and 75 key results to monitor.

Such a large number of objectives and key results is too much! Implemented this way, the OKR model increased the number of objectives to follow and created no clarity at all. Nobody knew what they really needed to follow and what to prioritize. Some of the objectives contradicted each other and neither support nor assistance was received for the resolution of any conflicts. A representative of the company we interviewed speculated that the biggest failure in implementing the OKR model was simply the number of things to follow.

Our own experience also confirms that it is a common fallacy that everyone should monitor all possible key results. The transparency of the OKR model means that all objectives and key results are visible to everyone. However, that does not mean that each person has to monitor all of them.

Once a team's objectives are derived from corporate-level objectives, the team has the freedom to focus on its own activities. Even the leadership team doesn't have to worry about all the key results of the entire organization all the time; each team is responsible for their own. That is what brings peace and clarity to work.

As this example story shows, the maximum number of objectives and key results is often too much. Already following 25 key results — not to mention 75 key results — requires resources that many organizations don't have. It is better to choose a few objectives and get them done — and emphasize to the team that it should only follow its own objectives, not all of them.]

How to identify frustration

How does a leader know that the staff lacks resources and employees are frustrated? One sign may be that workers deliver everything in the nick of time or late. Emails are sent out in the evenings, weekends and on holidays.

Resource shortages can also be observed in that tasks are left undone or are poorly done. The mistakes are caused by being in a hurry, which indeed is a contributing factor. The more things are in progress simultaneously and the more dispersed the focus, the more mistakes are made and the more things are forgotten.

In spoken language, frustration is observed in phrases like: "Damn it, this was also due today.", "Sorry, I totally missed the fact that you wanted the report back today?", "I took a quick stab at it last night.", "I just finished filling it out.", "I didn't really have time to dive deep into this." and "I'll try to get to it tomorrow."

How can frustration be avoided?

In the implementation of the OKR model, it is very important to have a dialogue about objectives: The leadership team has a conversation with managers and managers engage in conversation with their teams. Teams discuss objectives together.

You have to be realistic about setting objectives. If the workload is such that the OKRs are allocated no more than an hour per day; the objectives must be such that they can be completed over a few hours during one week. To get to this, the entire organization needs to learn honesty and transparency and start letting go of hero worship. They can no longer idolize those who make miracles happen at the expense of their well-being. Change has to be sustainable.

Frustration is eased when the leadership team shares that it has found the workload is too high relative to the resources. In the implementation project, it is worth emphasizing that the objective of adopting the OKR model is above all, to create clarity of work for the quarter and to give the possibility to focus — not to achieve more. It is important to track the development of the workload after the first quarter.

The implementation of the OKR model itself being the first OKR objective is also valuable. Since learning, communication, target setting, tracking and development of the OKR system all take time; it is quite realistic to set the objective of the first quarter solely on implementing the OKR model. This is already plenty of work in addition to daily tasks.

The implementation of the OKR model requires work, especially from managers. To avoid managers becoming frustrated you need to remove something from their normal workload because the OKR model will influence their management practices and routines. In addition, managers need to learn how to train people in OKR theory, facilitate objectives and support people during the change.

How to get over frustration

If it is discovered that none of the objectives are anywhere near the target, after the first follow-up period, it is necessary to discuss the workload in a brutally honest but gentle manner. At the same time, this is a reason to be happy, because the OKR model has just made the unsustainable and unproductive workload visible, and now you can begin to fix the issue.

There is a fear that by focusing on only one thing, a person isn't as productive and necessary as they used to be. It seems illogical that by doing fewer things at once you actually get more done. While in the manufacturing industry the benefits of limiting work in progress have long been known, expert work still lags far behind.

If you make the implementation of the OKR model the objective of the second quarter as well you get off to an even better start with the system. The results begin to speak for themselves as the amount of work becomes appropriate to the working time available.

In communication, it should be emphasized that the effectiveness of the entire organization improves when focusing on a few important issues at a time. Communication can use images such as those in this chapter and emphasize that it is more important to finish things than to start things.

If you want to learn more about flow efficiency, you should read **Eliyahu M. Goldratt's** *The Goal*, or **Gene Kim**, **Kevin Behr**, and **George Spafford's** *The Phoenix Project*.

6.6 No plan means you are treading in place

Vision ⊕ Concensus ⊕ Skills ⊕ Incentives ⊕ Resources ⊕	⊖ Treadmill

When the action plan is missing, the end result is a treadmill.

The last valley of death in the Lippitt-Knoster transformational leadership model relates to the lack of an action plan. This is rarely a problem with OKR implementation projects, as more often than not, organizations are used to making project plans. Occasionally though, you run into a situation where the organization seems to be running in place and stops making progress. This phenomenon is referred to as the treadmill.

The situation develops into a treadmill when there is no decent plan to implement the OKR model. On a treadmill the pace is awesome, and a lot of things are done all the time, but the organization is not actually progressing anywhere. This is what happens if you get the project off the ground, but do not have enough time to build support elements. These elements include communication and tracking plans, as well as retrospectives and feedback events.

The greatest treadmill effect comes when the key results do not tell you of the progress towards the objective and the daily tasks are not related to key results. In this case, new objectives and key results will be made quarterly, but daily work will continue unchanged.

How can you identify the treadmill?

The treadmill can be identified by the fact that at the end of the quarter, the OKRs have not progressed in the right direction. It may be that a lot of things have progressed a bit, but the objective has not moved forward significantly, or at all.

When you look at the results after the implementation period, you see that something completely different from what was recorded in the OKRs has been the focus. In this case, "something more important" or "something mandatory" has surfaced, or it was erroneously believed that the work was related to the OKR objective, but the selected key results show no progress.

When it is found that the implementation of the OKR model has not been successful, it is important that the implementation is again the main objective of the following quarter. The danger in this situation is that if nothing changes: key results and tasks will not be studied in relation to the previous quarter, the workload of the organization will not be lightened and people will continue running on a treadmill.

Three months later, the situation remains the same, the same debate happens and the situation does not improve. You can never implement the OKR model on a treadmill.

How can the treadmill be avoided?

Just because we've stressed throughout the book that the most important thing is to start doing and over-planning is detrimental, it doesn't mean that it's not necessary to have a plan. The plan, like the whole OKR model, is iterative and will be changed when flaws are discovered. Yet without a plan and discipline, there will be no improvements.

On company and team levels you need to know the answers to at least these questions:
- Where are OKRs recorded? (See Section 4.3 *OKR-software and systems.*)
- How often and when will the progress of OKRs be tracked? (See Section 3.5 *OKR tracking.*)
- How often and when will key metrics be updated?
- Who is tracking the OKRs?
- When and how will the next quarter be planned? (See Section 3.3 *Planning short-term for a quarter.*)
- Who needs to be contacted if your numbers don't change?

Once these are in the clear, the treadmill should not be an issue. It is essential to know who's doing something, when it's being done and what is being done. That's how to get started. The plan, support structures, processes and progression will be modified when results come in.

Clearly communicating how the deployment of OKRs should be reflected in the everyday life of work is also paramount. The following questions help with that:
- How does the implementation of OKRs affect other activities?
- Who is responsible for the change and who will track it?
- Where do people get support for their own activities?

When people know what an OKR model should look like, they can more quickly detect when actions do not match the plan.

How to get off the treadmill?

We have witnessed a few OKR implementations, where the plan has been non-existent. When it is not clear how it should be done, vague guidelines such as "each unit is responsible for deploying itself" have been used. An example of this where, as a result, one organization had nine different interpretations of the OKR model, meant it was not possible to form an overall picture.

It's never too late to go back to the drawing board and deal with the whole situation one step at a time. The first step is aligning the practices on:
- How to plan a quarter
- How to limit the amount of interpretation
- Where and how are objectives and key results recorded?
- What is the length of the implementation period?
- How do OKRs integrate with weekly meetings and other management structures?

The treadmill can also be discussed within the team; for example, by asking 'why?' *at least* five times:
- Why haven't the key results been fulfilled?
- Why is this the case?
- What causes problems or slowdowns?
- Why is it so?

On the fifth question, we begin to approach the root of the problem.

Discipline is the most important element of successful change, as change over a long time lasts a long time. Therefore, it is better to have five incomplete quarters than one perfect quarter. In our experience, the benefits will only begin to materialize after about a year, as you move from implementation towards managed work.

6.7 Summary and what's next

In this chapter, we have covered the most typical mid-stage death valleys of OKR deployment projects by using the Lippitt-Knoster change management model.

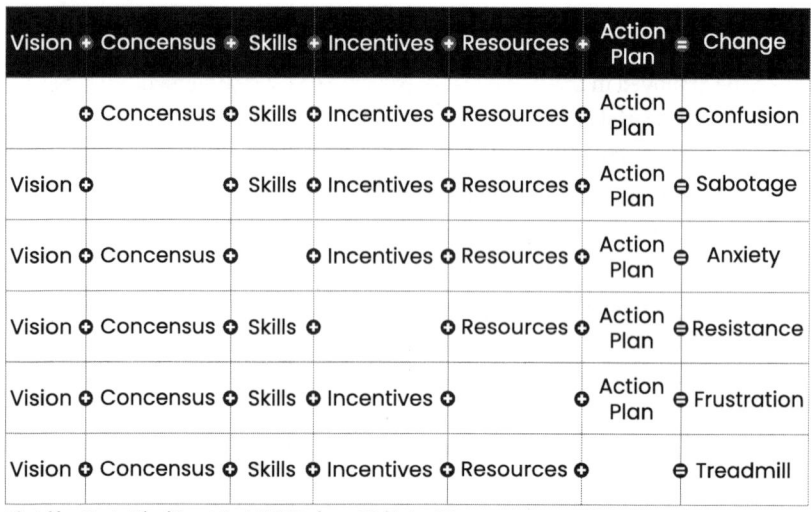

Vision +	Concensus +	Skills +	Incentives +	Resources +	Action Plan	=	Change
	⊕ Concensus ⊕	Skills ⊕	Incentives ⊕	Resources ⊕	Action Plan	⊖	Confusion
Vision ⊕		Skills ⊕	Incentives ⊕	Resources ⊕	Action Plan	⊖	Sabotage
Vision ⊕	Concensus ⊕		Incentives ⊕	Resources ⊕	Action Plan	⊖	Anxiety
Vision ⊕	Concensus ⊕	Skills ⊕		Resources ⊕	Action Plan	⊖	Resistance
Vision ⊕	Concensus ⊕	Skills ⊕	Incentives ⊕		⊕ Action Plan	⊖	Frustration
Vision ⊕	Concensus ⊕	Skills ⊕	Incentives ⊕	Resources ⊕		⊖	Treadmill

Adapted from Knoster, T (1991) Presentation in TASH Conference, Washington, D.C.
Adapted by Knoster from Enterprise Group, Ltd.

The complex change management model, adapted from the Lippitt-Knoster model.

The valley of death can be avoided by keeping the following in mind:
- The vision will be clear when you explicitly communicate why the OKR model is being implemented.
- Consensus is achieved when people are allowed to participate in decision-making.
- Necessary skills can be taught and brought into the organization for the implementation of the OKR model.
- Incentives are benefits to working life; such as clarity, focus and job prioritization - all of which the OKR model will bring.
- Too many resources, especially time, is always better than too few resources.
- A stable action plan helps everyone know what is being done, why it is being done, who is doing it and when they are doing it.

If these six perspectives have been taken into account in the implementation project and continue to be reviewed regularly, the transformational leadership of implementing the OKR model will succeed. All sorts of smaller pitfalls and inconveniences will still occur along the way. They will be conquered with continuous open discussions between the various teams and employees of the organization.

Up to this point in the book, the assumption has been that OKRs have been or will be deployed in the organization quite soon. The next chapter focuses on how, after the initial enthusiasm and the mid-project valley of death, the new normal will look. The chapter goes through the conditions needed for the OKR model to continue to work successfully. Finally, we'll learn how the OKR model behaves during a sudden crisis.

7 WHAT HAPPENS AFTER THE INITIAL IMPLEMENTATION?

After the implementation of the OKR model, many things within the organization are likely to change. Previous chapters have outlined the changes needed in processes and culture to get the model running. To get started, the organization needs to adopt a new kind of discipline, create new tracking models, choose a new tracking system, learn how to make exciting objectives and numeric key results and so on.

The change does not end there; even bigger changes are likely to come. The changes might occur as a byproduct of the OKR model, almost without effort, or they may require frank and honest discussions. The OKR model will eventually be incorporated into all management systems and it will affect both performance reviews as well as bonus models. In addition, it has an impact on the psychological safety of the organization and the amount of autonomy it has.

If all of these are concerns at the onset, there may be no progress at all. Bonus systems and performance reviews for example, might be so well established that the need to change them might already by itself kill the implementation of the whole OKR model.

We recommend reading this chapter only after the OKR model has already been implemented. If some of these come up at the start of the project, don't get bogged down in the details for too long. Whilst these are big issues they are not impossible to overcome.

You should be aware that any organization using the OKR model is never done with changes. The system needs to be able to repair itself to remain useful. Fortunately, the basic idea of the whole OKR model is that through continuous discussion, experimentation and learning, the best solution to any challenge will eventually be found.

This chapter examines what happens in an organization over time, once the OKR model is implemented. The chapter also goes through what to do in a crisis. When the OKR model is in place and the organization faces a surprising challenge, it is good to know how to change direction mid-quarter and how to react to the new situation without breaking routines and processes created with the OKR model.

7.1 Common cadences bring structure

Discipline in the OKR model has been talked about in this book; in the context of planning, tracking and communication. It is worth talking about it a little more because disciplined and systematic actions are necessary in the OKR model.

When OKR literature talks about discipline it is often linked to the cadence, the rhythm of actions. Some organizations are intrinsically good at it, some take longer to find their rhythm. What is essential about maintaining a cadence is that the chosen rhythm is maintained. OKRs are tracked and updated rigorously ; whether or not you feel like it , or whether you are busy with something more urgent. In a disciplined organization, the management system is extremely systematic.

The leadership team must bear mutual responsibility for ensuring that matters are dealt with systematically. If an organization has a habit of starting new things but not turning them into practices; maintaining mutual responsibility is even more important. Each team must ensure it is taking responsibility for its own OKRs. If passing the management review is easy; there is a lack of goal-orientation in the organization, which in turn means that the leadership team is also not being goal-oriented.

If there is no time allocated for tracking and updating OKRs and they are not enforced, there is also no time for focus and objectives. In these cases, you should take a step back and think about how these are supposed to be achieved in the first place. Good intentions often stay as mere intentions and are caused by the conflict between a grand plan and non-existent available time.

It would be ideal if management practices existed even before the OKR model — whether it is a Monday meeting of a small organization or a collection of leadership efforts in a large and complex organization. Managing objectives and key results should be integrated into these practices.

If a company does not yet have a systematic management system, the OKR model makes it possible to implement one. Results will be achieved if the company wants to develop in a more systematic direction and the teams can operate in a disciplined manner.

It's important to know what good looks like and what should be tried next in order to get to that. In several organizations, measuring performance has only started after the implementation of OKRs. Once you realize that work has not been very quantifiable, the need to create new metrics to support operations becomes apparent.

The use of suitable OKR software supports efficiency and discipline. A lot of software reminds teams and individuals to update their figures each week. Whilst some direct people to plan their weekly objective orientations all show the situation in real-time. The core of the OKR model is all about numbers, which have to change every week.

Discipline will be fueled by the changing numbers, starting a positive trend. Seeing numbers change and things moving in the right direction is rewarding. Regular discussions become supportive and motivating events and so habits become routine and a part of the natural cadence of operations.

7.2 The OKR model belongs in the annual clock

One key tool of a systematic organization is the annual clock. When an annual clock or other similar full-year calendar exists, it is easy to incorporate events of the OKR model as part of it. In a publicly listed company the annual clock is, of course, mandatory. If a company doesn't have an annual clock in place, now is a good time to create one.

The annual clock is a visualization of the year, where all relevant events for the company are marked down. These may include, for example:
- The Annual and Quarterly Planning Schedule (OKR Model)
- Joint staff events and meetings
- Major industry events and important dates
- Beginning and end dates of periods, seasons and other time periods of the industry
- Holiday periods and other exceptional periods
- Audits, important deadlines.

Now, the entire calendar year gets a cadence which helps pace the year as the focus of the annual clock is longer than just the next quarter. In addition, it also serves as a means of communication. The leadership team will be able to demonstrate its preparedness and show what is important over the next year.

Adhering to the annual clock and the planning cadence is essential. There is nothing more frustrating than painstakingly creating an annual clock at the beginning of the year and then seeing it not have any bearing on operations.

As soon as the implementation of the OKR model has progressed beyond the first quarter, the full-year calendar must be planned. The annual clock will include events related to the management system and the planning events of the OKR model for the full year. OKR tracking must be in the company's calendar for at least the next quarter. If possible, the meetings should be scheduled in the calendar for the entire year.

When events are in the calendar on time, there are no surprises and things get taken care of in time. This also ensures the benefits of parallel planning.

CASE: Motiva's strategic annual clock is built in Plandisc

Motiva is the national sustainability organization of Finland. It provides public and private sector operators, as well as consumers, with information and services that enable them to make resource-efficient, impactful and sustainable choices. Motiva decided to implement the OKR model and have it as a part of the annual clock in early 2020.

In the past, Motiva's operations have been guided traditionally with a plan derived from strategy. CEO **Vesa Silfver** saw the need to increase tracking, shorten planning cycles and shift the focus from analyzing historical metrics to working towards objectives that shape the future. In addition, he wanted the organization to see what is important right now and what is relevant to everyday working life.

Motiva's management team familiarized themselves with the OKR model and it seemed like a good fit. Motiva decided to boldly start experimenting with a quarterly cycle consistent with the OKR model and continually develop its activities based on the experience. Implementing the tracking cadence of the OKR model immediately as part of the annual clock was a central building block. The annual clock was created using the Plandisc tool.

The annual clock of Motiva in Plandisc.

From the beginning of the year, Motiva synchronized their annual clock to the OKR model. The annual clocks of the management team, board and staff alike now follow the quarterly cadence of the OKR model. This allows Silfver to have the necessary information from the staff before every board meeting. In the meeting, he will be able to report the situation of both sales and the OKRs to the board.

At Motiva, OKR tracking is done continuously in the TEAMS Planner, which all staff have access to. The progress of key results is tracked monthly once per quarter, a more thorough review is done.

Objectives and key results are essential content at board meetings and progress is also tracked at business line meetings. The annual clock and the OKRs are a natural part of Motiva's internal communication. In addition, with the introduction of the common annual clock and the OKR model, the organization has been able to align its activities and accelerate the process of bringing the strategy to daily work.

7.3 OKRs will be used in all operations

Over time, the OKR model will be implemented into as many company functions as possible. The more functions use the OKR model, the more you benefit from it. This should be easy because if the objectives are sufficiently exciting, people will talk about them, refer to them and display them proudly.

As noted in Section 3.1 *The cadence of planning and doing*, a company always has some form of annual planning. Once the OKR model has been implemented, OKRs will be a result of the annual planning. The OKR model is used to implement the company strategy, which is overseen by the board. Consequently, the situation of objectives and key results should be reported to the Board at every meeting. These are basic practices.

Once the basics are in place, you might want to innovate more ways to use OKRs in your management practices. For example, the company's monthly info sharing or similar communications and their materials could be organized in accordance with the OKRs. This would highlight the importance of the objectives and guide you to talk about important issues every time. If something does not fall under the headlines from the OKRs, it might be irrelevant. Either it is not worth talking about — or the OKRs need to be updated.

The OKR model should be an essential part of onboarding. New employees should immediately be taught the basics of the OKR model and learn the main objectives of the year for the company. This way, new employees immediately understand what the company is aiming at for the year. At the same time, the language of the OKR model also becomes familiar.

Things stay in mind better when the objectives and key results are visual. In section 4.3.2 *OKRs on a whiteboard – case study Labrox*, we saw how Labrox's objectives and key results are on the wall of the company office. This way OKRs are always on the minds of people passing by. It's also easy to gather around the board to discuss.

Objectives can be printed as a poster or as a board for the company wall. In addition to being visible in BetterWorks, Futurice's OKR targets can be seen, as printed boards on the office walls. In a digitalized world, the role of analog communication is not to be forgotten. Alongside the objectives themselves, questions and encouragements relating to the OKRs can be put on the walls.

On the other hand, software also generates different views and compositions of OKRs. These can be used as a rolling presentation, for example, on a TV screen in the coffee room, on the information screens in the hallways, or a large screen in the company's lobby, so that it can be seen by everyone as they come to work in the morning. Futurice also has an information display in which real-time OKR data is visible to everyone.

The OKR model can be made part of every day in several different ways. The only limit is your imagination.

CASE: Weekdone has a built-in TV dashboard

OKR software Weekdone has a television view that can be run on all the company's information screens. Weekdone keeps its OKRs visible on a TV screen placed in their canteen.

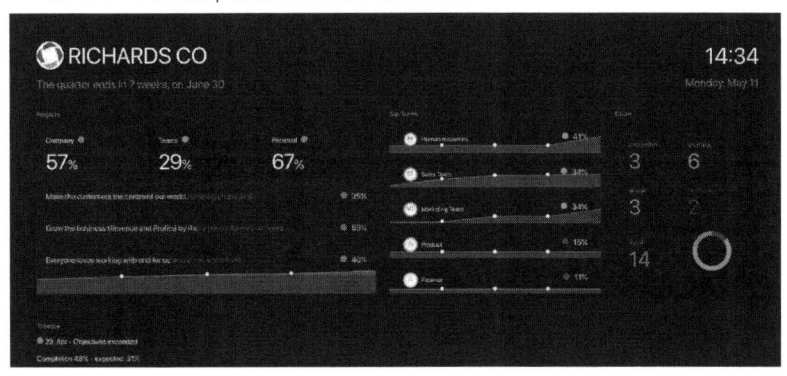

An example of the infoscreen view in WeekDone.

CASE: Values are memorized, OKRs not

Heltti is a well-being and health services company, aimed especially at expert workers. CEO **Timo Lappi** describes Heltti as a self-organized ball pit organization. Heltti is a heavily value-driven TEAL organization with both OKRs and KPIs in use.

In Heltti, employees must understand and remember the company's values — preferably by heart. They control the daily activities of employees, and therefore, attention has been paid to internalizing them. Lappi has, for example, implemented a value bingo in which he randomly asks his employees for company values. The people of Heltti do well in bingo.

OKRs don't have to be memorized in Heltti. It is acceptable to forget, at a corporate level or even at a team level, what the exact wording or content of the OKRs are. What is more pertinent is knowing where the objectives and key results can be found and making sure to guide activities at a weekly level. In addition, people only need to follow their own and their team's objectives to know how their work affects the achievement of objectives.

It is quite normal to begin the week by examining what the tasks of the week are. If work is planned and derived from OKRs, employees can rely on their daily task list. It's exhausting and near useless to try to memorize all the OKRs all the time. Values on the other hand, will always remain the same, so knowing and committing them to memory makes more sense.]

7.4 Rewards and OKRs

One of the most challenging topics in implementing the OKR model is rewarding mechanisms, since there should be no monetary bonuses tied to OKR targets. We are used to encouraging people through money and rewarding desirable behavior with financial bonuses. Many organizations have performance rewards in place that are difficult or impossible to dismantle because they are linked to remuneration.

The fundamental, unequivocal principle of the OKR model is that financial rewards are not bound to OKRs. Monetary rewards don't work with stretch targets. This doesn't mean that the OKR model cannot be implemented if the company has a performance rewarding method that is unable to be dismantled.

The coordination of the OKR model and bonuses is made in a way that the objectives and key results recorded in the OKR model indicate the direction in which the organization wants to go, based on the strategy. Bonuses are, in turn, paid for achieving desired results but not for objectives themselves.

For example, if an organization has ambitious growth targets, they are usually measured by revenue and earnings. Bonuses are paid based on revenue and earnings numbers, but these figures are not OKR key results. The OKRs will promote growth and support them and the achievement of which contributes to revenue and earnings. These objectives may include improving customer satisfaction, acquiring new customers, developing new services or reducing the number of reclamations. These objectives are to achieve the desired growth but are not financially incentivised directly.

In this case, OKRs and bonuses steer activity in the same direction and the systems can coexist. If bonuses are paid for objectives that conflict with OKRs, money always wins - this is natural. Therefore, it should be ensured that bonuses and OKRs steer teams in the same direction.

CASE: Nixu rewards based on financial figures

Cybersecurity company Nixu's operations are driven by strategy and both OKRs and KPIs. The company's strategy strongly demonstrates the direction that one wants to go toward. OKRs are a tool for implementing and managing the defined strategy. Objectives and key results determine the operative outputs and OKRs make the organization objective-oriented. OKRs are not a basis for financial rewards.

The KPI metrics, on the other hand, demonstrate the financial outcome of operations. The KPIs are completely separate from the OKRs and demonstrate the so-called hard facts. Incentives are tied specifically to KPIs and are tracked biannually in development discussions.

At Nixu, no conflict has been found between KPI figures that offer financial rewards and OKRs that inspire. For example, a certain sales figure may be a KPI, but at the same time the OKR goal may be to increase the sales rate of a particular product or service. These do not contradict, but support each other.]

Personal OKRs and rewards

As highlighted in Section 2.2.6 *Objectives are set at the team level*, OKRs are generally worthwhile only on the team level, so that OKRs contribute to teamwork. However, there are plenty of organizations that use personal OKRs and they might be one of the factors on which a person's performance within an organization is measured.

OKRs are a relevant topic of discussion when assessing an individual's performance and work contribution within an organization yet they cannot be a mathematical metric in evaluating human performance. OKRs are in principle, not a metric, but a desired result. Secondly, OKRs can rarely be compared.

Take, for example, two people with personal OKRs. The first of them, Pete , negotiates his objectives over several sessions with his manager, coming out with key results that he knows he will easily achieve. At the end of the quarter, Pete's numbers are 125% of the target.

John, on the other hand, manages to develop a tough, but inspiring stretch objective for himself. Reaching 100 percent performance in a quarter is grueling work. At the end of the quarter, John has achieved 70 percent of his target but has contributed to the company's strategic objectives significantly with his work.

If the achievements are mathematically calculated with the formula "reward = performance rate of objectives", Pete, who negotiated the easier objective, will get a higher reward. John, who has furthered the company's strategy, is getting less money to take home. This is unfair.

Furthermore, it has to be taken into account that when OKRs lead change, it pushes people outside of their comfort zone and forces them to learn. For some, it is easier than for others. For one individual, some changes can be easy to implement, for others it is more difficult. Therefore, stretch objectives and the impact of the results on the individual and the company vary depending on the situation.

Achieving OKRs may be one component in assessing a person's performance, but there should always be an interpretation of the objectives by the manager. They cannot solely be valued mathematically. The manager should note how a person runs his objectives, maintains them and learns based on them. There is no mathematical formula for this, it is based on monitoring and judgment by the manager.

Sales OKRs

Sales OKRS are a particularly difficult issue. Sales commission is not just part of the compensation, but often a reason for choosing the field. Many salespeople are entrepreneurial and the direct impact of their own work on the level of income is one of the biggest reasons to stay in the industry and the job. So, the OKR targets of the sales department are one of the most challenging aspects in the adoption of the OKR model.

With sales OKRs, it is strongly recommended that you don't try to solve this challenge immediately as this may become a roadblock and the whole project will fail before any benefit from the OKR model is obtained. Another recommendation is that sales metrics are not used directly as objectives, but rather kept separate like bonuses.

Sales metrics are the result of a type of work commission tied specifically to that work, so OKRs should be tied to developing the work that leads to results. Some sample OKRs for sales could be:

- Contact customers of a specific profile.
- Increase the number of customer calls.
- Create a new lead generation campaign with marketing.
- Speed up the sales cycle from contact to sale.
- Participate in new sales training.

These objectives support and help sales achieve business objectives but are not directly rewarded. You can very well put some stretch on them because the more customers the salesperson contacts or the more lead generation campaigns are running, the more likely it is that the sales target will be met. Similarly, the sales team's activities are planned to align with strategic objectives. If the strategic objective is to conquer a new market, then contacting customers in that market will be an objective. But the sales commission remains unaffected.

This all sounds simple, but in practice there are often challenges with sales OKRs. Sales often question the OKR model because salespeople are accustomed to guiding their work themselves through sales objectives. It is difficult to clarify the importance of OKRs, especially if the company tries to maintain "hard" revenue targets and "inspiring" OKR targets simultaneously. This juxtaposition is discussed in more detail in section 7.7 *Financial objectives and OKRs*.

It is important that salespeople understand the role that OKRs have in guiding operations strategically. Their implementation will help sales reach their objectives. OKRs must not conflict with sales targets or salespeople could easily reject the OKRs after the first conflict.

7.5 OKRs will impact your performance reviews

Performance reviews are a fairly established practice in a lot of companies. A typical performance review takes place once a year, with a lot of expectations loaded into it. This encounter is often wrapped up in an assessment of job performance, mutual feedback between manager and employee, as well as a compensation discussion. A year's worth of expectations culminates in an hour-long meeting;the results are collected in a document that will be buried in the HR system and in the worst case, only opened when the next performance review begins.

From the perspective of the OKR model, the problem points in the performance review are obvious. With the traditional model, a person's objectives are not tied to OKRs AND they are often left too detached from the actual work and are not followed up on often enough. As the OKR model guides an organization toward continuous development, rapid learning and objective-oriented activities, an ongoing discussion with managers is needed to support personal growth. Having only one annual meeting between the employee and their manager is no longer sufficient.

Moreover, the traditional performance review is plagued by oversized expectations and excessive ceremony. The performance review season is often solemnly launched with an announcement by the manager and the process involves filling out various forms. This creates a rigid and distant impression of the whole event from the start and the employee anticipates the moment when it is time to discuss compensation throughout the discussion.

Ceremony only fuels oversized expectations. The expectation pile-up is further compounded by the emphasis on the importance of the performance review. The person's employment for the whole year is reviewed, which is a huge effort, as there may have been a lot to go through from the year. Sadly, the results of many performance reviews do not often have any impact on the activities of the employee or the manager.

Changing performance reviews in an organization, let alone ending them, is not an easy task, especially if you are used to them and the employees await these events. Similarly, in organizations where performance reviews have not been held so far, it may be a difficult task to initiate such a thing. Whichever the situation, it is simply impossible for many organizations to switch to a different practice than it is used to. Again, expectation management is important.

It is not the intent of the OKR model to scrap performance reviews. Instead, the purpose is to improve the interaction between the manager and the employee, and change the performance reviews organically. With the implementation of the OKR model, the interaction becomes more frequent and more immediate than it previously was.

What happens to performance reviews?

While performance reviews can rightly be criticized for excessive ceremony, we don't believe that all ceremonies are bad. Routine brings security and people enjoy some rituals. Even after the OKR implementation, at least one yearly event is required to focus on the future and to update the objectives for the role as well as personal objectives. In these meetings, it is useful to discuss what has been achieved, how it has been achieved and how the tasks of the role are handled.

Even though objectives and key results give visibility to achieving objectives, the OKR model does not calculate personal performance. One person's 20 percent OKR performance can be made up of much more effort than someone else's 80 percent performance. Objectives cannot be measured or compared with the same metrics.

A manager's judgment is needed to evaluate performance — don't rely only on key results. It is also necessary to still have compensation and feedback discussions and the appropriate medium for them may still be something akin to a development review.

Once the OKR model is implemented, a change in the cadence of communication between the manager and employee about objectives and key results moves from annual to more frequent and ongoing conversations happening throughout the year. The manager is more knowledgeable about the learning objectives of the employee, the development targets and the obstacles. In the OKR model, a culture of instant feedback is needed. In this culture, an individual's good or bad performance is is quickly responded to in order to facilitate learning

It is good to consider how performance reviews are compatible with the OKR model and how they can be developed in your organization. For example, it is good to consider whether performance reviews need to be centrally managed. What is the role and purpose of the review in relation to the management system of the company? How can the nature of performance reviews change as OKRs and autonomy evolve?

Solution models from moderate change to blowing up the whole system

1. Keep performance reviews as before.
2. Keep performance reviews, but synchronize the follow-up to the OKR cadence.
3. Keep the performance reviews; but keep the focus of the discussion on the role, success and growth of the individual.
4. Keep performance reviews, but tie skills development to people's personal OKRs. Follow them quarterly.
5. Drop performance reviews and replace them with the Reaktor model.
6. Drop performance reviews and use the CFR model.

From performance reviews to development planning — the Reaktor model

The IT industry consultancy house, Reaktor, has career growth discussions in place of performance reviews, and are using neither managers nor HR to facilitate them. Reaktor's flat organization lacks direct managers, which explains why no traditional performance review model has been implemented. Also, managing performance reviews for an international company employing hundreds of people would be an impossible task for HR to do alone.

Reactor explains the model in the following way: "Career growth planning is a tool for professional development and bringing focus to objectives. A manager may not always be the most appropriate expert available."

Reaktor uses the terms sparrer and sparring. The sparrer can either be a mentor, an expert in the same field, or a coach - that is a professional facilitator.

In career growth discussions both participants explore directions for personal development, development of work, new technologies and methods, or other topics that are relevant for career development. Based on one or more of these discussions, a personal development plan will be made.

In the Reaktor model, discussions about pay and job evaluation are separated from planning. There is a desire to distinguish between competence development and the evaluation of performance. The Reactor development planning model has been made publicly available and can be downloaded from https://growthdiscussions.reaktor.com/en/.

Conversations, feedback, and recognition — Using the CFR model as a supplement of OKRs

In the OKR model, reflecting and learning are important. The culture of continuous feedback and reflection is quite natural in many companies and may not require adopting a model. It is important that the conversations, as well as the requesting and receiving of feedback are systematic. A culture of continuous feedback does not appear from thin air and learning does not occur unless time is made for it.

If you are only starting with feedback and reflection, the CFR model can help. CFR stands for conversations, feedback and recognition. In **John Doerr's** book *Measure What Matters* the CFR model is presented as an integral part of the OKR model. They support each other and CFR is in many ways an extension of the OKR model.

CFR is intended to be a tool for managers that eliminates traditional performance reviews and replaces them with continuous feedback. CFR conversations are separate from compensation discussions and their purpose is first and foremost to bolster coaching — not give orders.

CFR events are held during and especially at the end of each OKR implementation cycle. The CFR is a face-to-face meeting in which objectives are reviewed, realizations are reflected on and progress forward is discussed.

C — Conversations

Conversations take place both during and at the end of the OKR cycle. Topics depend on what point the cycle is at.

Typical questions between a manager and an employee during the implementation period include:

1. How are your OKRs progressing?
2. What skills do you need in order to succeed with your objectives?
3. Do you have anything that prevents your objectives from being reached?
4. Is there a need to change anything in your OKRs? Do they need to be edited, amended or reduced?
5. What feedback would you give regarding my or the organization's actions?

At the end of the implementation period, the topics for discussion may be:

1. We achieved the goal: what factors contributed to this?
2. We did not achieve the goal: what obstacles impacted our achievement?
3. Was the goal trickier or easier to achieve than we assumed?
4. What have we learned from this implementation period? What do we need to take into account when the next one begins?
5. What feedback would you give regarding my or the company's actions?

F — Feedback

Feedback is an integral part of CFR. It is requested between conversations and creates an opportunity for an employee to provide feedback to the organization and manager and for the manager to give feedback to his employee, ideally face-to-face.

A lot of different rules, instructions and templates have been written regarding feedback, for example, *Thanks for the Feedback* by **Sheila Heen** and

Douglas Stone. Also, feedback models such as the FBI or SBI, can help in formulating feedback.

The FBI comes from *Feeling, Behavior,* and *Impact and* SBI stands for *Situation, Behavior,* and *Impact*. What is important in both, is that feedback is given about one particular event that is clearly recalled. Feedback should be provided as soon as possible after what happened and should not be in the form of "you never…" or "you always…".

The feedback states the situation, how the recipient of feedback in the situation behaved, and what impact it had. The FBI version starts with what feeling the feedback recipient's behavior evoked in the feedback provider.

The idea behind both models is that the recipient of the feedback is not blamed for what happened, but feedback is told through the feedback provider's own experience and perspective. The FBI and SBI are based on *nonviolent communication*.

Here are a few common feedback practices:
- Be sure to give more positive than negative feedback.
- Separate positive and negative feedback.
- Do not use the hamburger or sandwich model where the critical feedback, the improvement and correction proposal, is sandwiched between positive feedback and praise.
- Always give feedback as quickly as possible after the event.
- Provide constructive feedback privately and give the feedback recipient enough time to ask clarifying questions.
- Make sure that the recipient gets to tell their side of the story.
- Most often, a person already knows they have done wrong and only needs support in admitting the mistake and in finding solutions.
- Be specific and help agree with clear development proposals that can be tracked or measured unequivocally.

R — Recognition

Recognition at and for work is important as a builder of trust and affection. Patrick Lencioni identifies in *Three Signs of a Miserable Job* three hallmarks of a miserable job: *anonymity, irrelevance and immeasurement*. According to Lencioni, employees generally do not feel fulfillment in their work unless their work is visible and relevant to others as well. When others — especially managers — notice their work and give credit for it, two out of three factors of misery disappear.

Recognition should not be spared, but given in abundance and whenever there is reason to. Recognition should be immediate and authentic. Each organization has slightly different ways of giving recognition, so each organization needs to follow what is right for them.

Giving recognition to a colleague
The organization should encourage recognition between employees. Recognition should not be a purely managerial job. Some people place significantly more weight on a colleague's recognition of their work, as colleagues see the work in practice and often understand its nature better.

Giving recognition in front of the team
The OKR model is team-oriented, so the individual may feel invisible. When an individual does his job well, the whole team needs to know. Feedback can be given simply by walking in on the team's weekly OKR check in and giving them the feedback. The forum already exists, and the relevant people are there.

Sharing recognition on a Organizational level
Organizations often have a variety of internal communication forums, such as an intranet, instant messaging, or an email newsletter. Sharing recognition of a job well done to the whole organization is pretty inexpensive and easy. Sure, some perceive overly public feedback as awkward or even negative. However, feedback in writing does not put anyone in too much of a spotlight and public recognition still feels good.

CFR aligns with the OKR model

John Doerr considers the CFR model to be downright essential to the success of the OKR model. However, when we have interviewed Finnish companies using the OKR model, we have noticed that few use CFR. Although the strategy is brought into everyday life by the OKR model, the CFR model has not been adopted.

This may be because the OKR model has been freshly implemented and there is still a lot of work left to bring it into daily working life. Another reason may be that performance reviews have such a powerfully institutionalized position. The more established practices are, the more difficult they are to break free of.

Whether or not the CFR model will be used in the company is not critical. It is more important to adopt some systematic, frequent communication model. It's essential to evaluate the past, learn about what's done, give feedback and look forward. CFR can be a good tool for it if there is no working model in place yet. If another model is already implemented and it works, there is no need to fix what isn't broken.

CASE: HappyOrNot ditches performance reviews for CFR model

HappyOrNot from Tampere specializes in collecting feedback on people's satisfaction. The company is known for its feedback delivery device for multi-customer service situations. The device allows the customer to assess the experience by using one of four different emoticons. In addition to the physical device, HappyOrNot measures the quality of the customer or employee experience online as well.

Eeva Lennon and **Heidi Hyysalo** from HappyOrNot explain that the company collects feedback regularly from its employees as well. Anonymous feedback keeps HappyOrNot well-informed about the general mood and satisfaction of staff. In addition, the company fosters ongoing and personal feedback discussions with the staff.

HappyOrNot has a strong one-to-one discussion culture in which personal conversations take place between an employee and a manager biweekly or even weekly. The implementation of the OKR model has also increased regular communication. OKRs have become a natural way of one-on-one discussions.

There is a very short distance from this to the CFR model, as CFR goes hand in hand with the OKR model. Where one-on-one conversations are more of a chance for the employee to get to tell his or her thoughts and feedback, CFR is a two-way conversation where feedback is given in both directions.

According to Lennon and Hyysalo, CFR's advantage is that it brings regularity and familiarity to the discussions — participants know what they are going to discuss. What is important is being present and having the opportunity to speak freely and openly.

HappyOrNot's CFR tempo is fast. Lighter CFR events are held weekly. In a short, less than half an hour-long, meeting, the manager will walk through the OKRs in the Sympa HR system. The manager organizes a longer meeting, just over half an hour, every month.

At the end of the quarter, there is a longer CFR discussion, which reflects on the past quarter and looks at the following quarter. The quarterly CFR events last from 45 minutes to an hour. The most thorough CFR events, lasting from one hour to two, are held twice a year. Teams can also have CFR discussions with other teams.

The term performance review is no longer used in HappyOrNot. Instead, an ongoing conversation between the employee and the manager makes sure that the employee and their job image develop. Lennon and Hyysalo have found that tracking and repetitive talking are essential acts to make things move from theory to practice.

7.6 Towards an autonomous organization

When the OKR model is first implemented, levels of autonomy do not have to be very high in the company. To reap the greatest possible benefit from the model it is beneficial, or even mandatory, to increase a team's autonomy. If the goal is not to increase the level of autonomy, it's worth thinking about whether to implement the model in the first place

Traditional, hierarchical, top-down management models do not generally create committed employees. Teams aren't motivated and it can feel like the leadership teamt is hovering overhead and their energy and time is spent supervising employees, distributing and controlling tasks. To reduce the leadership team's workload and stress, the organization as a whole must be able to focus on relevant activities and achieve results independently.

For a leadership team it means communicating the big picture, explaining the context of events, monitoring execution on a high level and providing assistance when necessary. It does not mean micromanaging task distribution and dictating operations. For employees, it means taking responsibility for their own job description and making independent decisions in their role.

An autonomous and self-guiding company produces better results than traditional models. As a result of autonomy, people's responsibility for strategy implementation will increase. Not only will the potential of the enterprise as a whole be more effectively deployed, but people's sense of purpose, as well as their motivation will be strengthened.

The book has previously mentioned Daniel Pink's *Drive: The Surprising Truth About What Motivates Us*. Its content is not only closely related to Sections 1.7 How finding purpose in work motivates people and 4.1.2 Why is the OKR model implemented? but also to the autonomous organization. Pink's book artfully explains why the OKR model affects both the purpose of work and autonomy.

Pink writes about motivational factors for individuals and how the current management and reward models of most organizations do not actually contribute to people's motivation or the desirability of a job. Autonomy in the OKR model is well-aligned with the points that Pink identifies as essential motivational factors: autonomy, mastery and purpose.

Autonomy

Autonomy is the ability to define the contents of one's own work or at least some of the objectives and ways of getting to them. This is exactly what the OKR model aims at. Even though the area of freedom when interpreting the objectives would first be limited, the ability and permission for teams to determine their own objectives will increase, see section 3.4.4 *The model develops alongside the organization*. Hierarchical organizations, where tasks are dictated and their execution is determined by someone else are the opposite of this.

Mastery

Mastery is the goal of becoming better and developing as an individual. People dabble in the most curious things because it's fun and they feel that they progress in them. The same need to learn and become a master also drives us at work. The OKR model removes the frustration that comes from nothing progressing and demands that people bring up blockers to progress and mastery so that they can be removed or alleviated.

Purpose

Purpose refers to the feeling that your work has a positive effect, other than providing pay or contributing to company performance. People wish to feel that through their work, they can influence the future of customers, society or the world positively. With the OKR model projects are completed and objectives are achieved. When their effects are purposeful, the job is too.

The OKR model can support a lot in achieving these three, especially autonomy. To increase autonomy, you first need to build trust. Trust improves not only by trusting others but also by being trustworthy. For management, it means that the team's autonomy should be increased gradually. If a team is to take responsibility, it must also be empowered.

For teams, building trust means that the teams are constantly working towards the objectives of the OKR model, reporting progression and learning about what they are doing. It is up to teams and individuals to ask for help if the desired objectives are not reached. You can't always succeed 100 percent. What is important, however, is to bring up difficult things promptly, discuss

the situation and agree on effective next steps. This is how mutual trust is built.

By tackling poor performance, the leadership team is signaling the importance of the issue. This improves morale and trust. r Those frustrated by the effects of poor performance on collaboration, receive a renewed faith in things to come. Continuously saying that we are "learning," while in reality key results have not been updated, help has not been requested and objectives have not been achieved in any way, is universally unacceptable.

As teams can take even more responsibility for their actions, the leadership team gains more freedom in their mission. A positive spiral ensues, leading to more independent activities and people committed to their work with a clear mission in mind.

7.7 Financial Objectives Management and the OKR Model

You cannot have two competing models in an organization: "hard" financial results and "nice" OKR targets. As we said in Section 7.4 *Rewards and OKRs*, if the two contradict each other, the OKRs will lose importance. If the financial objectives and OKRs are disconnected, people will circumvent the OKRs and work only towards financial objectives, which are always mandatory.

Both the financial objectives and the OKRs must steer operations in the same direction — together. Financial results are the result of the company's operations, so the OKRs should be formulated in a way that supports achieving the financial results.

For example, the goal of the year may be to better serve existing customers, so that they buy more services. Over the course of the year, enough of the right quarterly actions are done to make a meeting with existing clients a necessity. This improves customer satisfaction and loyalty and also helps achieve financial objectives.

In practice, it is possible to take into account financial objectives in the context of the OKR model in the following ways:

1. Financial objectives can be written directly as key results in OKRs,
2. Every planning event, as well as general communication, emphasizes that the OKRs are aligned towards strategic and economic objectives.

In the latter, the danger is that people over time will forget how the OKR targets relate to economic targets unless it has been properly recorded. This will cause the OKRs and financial objectives to diverge and for people to only focus on the financial objectives without the strategic and parallel guidance from the OKRs.

Financial objectives and OKRs are present in the OKR versus KPI debate. Often financial objectives are reflected in KPI metrics. However, there is no need to pay that much attention to the KPIs if the objectives are realized through the pursuit of the OKRs.

There is no single solution for managing financial objectives with the OKR model. The only common factor is that financial objectives cannot conflict with OKR targets. For example, if the objective is to make major changes in the operations of an organization with the same resource count as in the previous year, you have to accept that revenue and performance may be impacted. If objectives are not aligned, the organization will not devote enough time and energy to make the needed changes, but will only focus on implementing the financial objectives.

It is worth figuring out which activities and changes will best implement economic objectives in both the long term and the short term. Financial results are always the result of work well done and for improving that work, the OKR model is the best possible tool.

7.8 Changing OKRs in a crisis

The last, but certainly not least, issue in adopting the OKR model concerns preparation for crises and other surprising situations — whether threats or opportunities. One typical concern with autonomy-boosting systems is "What do you do in a sudden crisis?" What if, for example, a Lehman Brothers situation like the 2007 subprime crisis recurs and the organization only has a few hours to cope with the situation?

In some of the organizations, the leadership team retains a type of veto by mutual agreement. Under the agreement, leadership has the right and the opportunity to take full control for a moment and dictate the next steps, should something truly surprising happen.

This might increase the sense of security within the organization. Simon Sinek, for example, explains in his speech *Why Leaders Eat Last*, how leaders are given power precisely because when a crisis comes up, people know that the leaders will step up. According to Sinek, executives are allowed better benefits and higher salaries partially because they are expected to defend and protect the organization, as well as be the first responders.

Fortunately, we rarely encounter a major crisis or catastrophe in which there would be so little reaction time that you would need to change the operating model instantaneously. More often than not, the economic situation, the legislation, the competitive situation, or the market situation changes slowly enough to allow the organization to respond to it. Sometimes it can still happen and it is good to agree to a common process for crises in advance.

Whether it is a change that impedes operations or a new opportunity that emerges in the middle of the quarter and which management would like to seize, it can be reacted to in accordance with OKR principles. OKRs should be modified to reflect the new situation quickly, rather than doing things outside of OKRs — that is, leaving OKR targets lying around and just switching abruptly to doing something outside the OKRs. If you respond to a situation without adjusting the OKR model, it will be difficult for members of the organization to know what exactly is expected of them. The perception of what's most important blurs and teams, let alone individuals, no longer know what to focus on.

How do you change OKRs mid-quarter?

We want to once again stress that under normal circumstances OKRs should not be changed in the middle of a quarter, because otherwise, people will not be able to trust them in the future. If the objective set at the beginning of the quarter becomes secondary during the quarter, the work done until that point will seem unnecessary. Moreover, schedules and resources rarely allow trying to achieve more objectives with the same resources at the same time, contributing to inefficiency.

However, there are situations, crises or opportunities that you need to react to and you can't wait until the end of the quarter and the normal planning cycle. In this case, changing the OKRs during a quarter is justified. An about-turn in OKRs during the quarter can be reasonable and fully justified, for example, in the following situations:

- A pandemic threatens to ruin the company's finances.
- An equivalent of the bankruptcy of Lehman Brothers, which affects the global economy.
- A competitor unexpectedly releases a revolutionary product to the market.
- Production halts as a result of the destruction of a supplier's inventory

In such cases, a new planning cycle is initialized and it is determined which old objective this new objective displaces and what must wait until this new goal is implemented. A solution to a crisis can never add a sixth goal to the quarter and one of the previous objectives must be removed.

Changing OKRs requires discussion at every level of the organization: among the leadership team, between the leadership team and managers, between managers and employees, and between teams. In addition, it requires changing the personal objectives of everyone and replanning operations. This is expensive for an organization, and should not be done lightly.

In the case of an acute crisis in which there are only a few hours of response time, normal operations usually come to a halt and OKR discussions can be conducted at quite a fast pace. The focus should be on setting the big picture quickly and aligning people behind the new objective.

There is a need for the leadership team to believe in a systematic and disciplined course of action, including during times of uncertainty or rapid changes. It is important to understand the difference between agility and ad hoc. In the first, changes are made with a rapid cycle but still completed. In the latter, every impulse is reacted to and things are changed without a plan or cadence.

OKRs are a wonderful opportunity to connect the competence, know-how and innovativeness of the entire organization to problem-solving. When a situation is brought through the OKR system as the most important thing for the entire organization, everyone is working on ways to resolve it.

7.9 Covid changes organizations' OKRs

This book was already mostly written when the Covid-19 pandemic struck. Both the pandemic and the necessary safety measures have been tough on organizations. This was, and still is at the time of writing this, a crisis that required evaluating existing OKRs. Depending very much on the strategy of the company and the objectives derived from it, OKRs may have remained either completely unchanged or may have had to be partially or even completely replaced.

When we discussed covid with different organizations during the initial shock, many discussions highlighted the activation of manual control as a part of crisis management. In several organizations, the leadership team took a much more active role. There is an increased need for leadership to be active and set the direction in each decision that is required in a changed situation.

Investor and former CEO **Ben Horowitz** has described this shift in terms as a **peacetime CEO** and **wartime CEO**. A peacetime CEO focuses on increasing psychological safety, developing culture, and strengthening autonomous decision-making. A wartime CEO on the other hand, focuses on eradicating all obstinance and disagreements and overseeing the execution of the decided direction, even if they have to do it by giving direct orders.

In peacetime, the company is allowed to grow market share, fulfill its purpose, strengthen its culture, innovate and thrive. Wartime, on the other hand, refers to any situation in which the future of a company is threatened. For several companies, this pandemic and the subsequent recession may well require the introduction of a wartime CEO toolkit.

In any case, the relationship between the coronavirus and the OKR model is fundamentally very simple. Since the OKR model is a strategy derivative, you first need to check whether the pandemic has had a material impact on the company's strategy. It may be that because of the coronavirus, the whole strategy or parts of it have been rendered obsolete.

Usually, a set of assumptions are recorded in the strategy. Covid may knock down a large part of them. For example, an organization planning to conquer the US market will no longer be able to send its employees to that location. It inevitably follows that the organization needs to completely reassess what it is doing. This does not just mean reforming OKRs, but also scenario work on the whole strategy.

- Are we waiting for US flights to resume, or will we come up with a different approach in the meantime?
- How do we get digital sales to pick up, and what if they don't?
- What will presumably be the impact of the slump ahead on national and international trade making?

Once the strategic direction has been reviewed, a check will be made to see if the OKR targets change. If the strategic objectives have remained unchanged, the OKRs may also remain unchanged or change only partially. If, on the other hand, the central tenets of action are obsolete, the OKRs have also lost their relevance.

For example, the OKRs of a restaurant whose operations were temporarily shut down by a government decree are now obsolete. In such a situation, you have to think about what the objectives of the organization are and what to do when people are once again allowed inside the restaurant.

One manufacturing industry company continued virtually unchanged, even though all people had to switch to remote work. The situation led to a complete overhaul of the IT department's OKRs. Since everyone needed to telecommute and very quickly, these changes superseded the previous OKRs of the IT department. OKRs in other departments, however, remained exactly as they were before the onset of the pandemic. Once more is known about the effects and consequences of covid, they will be considered at the next quarterly planning event.

It may also be the case that OKR targets remain unchanged, but the situation requires rewriting key results and tasks. For example, many organizations have become accustomed to creating new customer contacts face to face. Physical appointments have been an integral part of a successful customer relationship and are, therefore, included in many key results. In the new situation, the entire purchase pipeline and deployment phase may have to be done digitally; radically changing the operating model and key results and tasks.

In several companies, covid-19 has led to a sudden dip in KPIs. The incoming requests have collapsed or there has been a significant decrease in the amount of billable work. This was the case for Elisa Heikura Ltd from section 2.2.6 *Objectives are set at the team level*, whose main income consists of on-site training and speaker engagements.

Elisa Heikura Ltd's strategic objectives - increasing awareness, consolidating and growing its customer base and developing products and services to be sold, have not changed as they are not directly affected by the pandemic. Thus, no changes had to be made to the OKRs.

In practice, however, the disappearance of billable work leads to a sudden change in priorities. First, you have to come up with ways to continue to implement the purpose of the organization so that existing customers are served and revenue is generated. Only then will there be a renewed focus on increasing awareness and developing services.

In the event of a sudden crisis, the order of action is, therefore:

- First, check how the situation affects the strategy and what possible scenarios the future holds.
- Next, see how the OKR targets serve the strategy under the changed circumstances.
- Then, check whether the selected key results are still the most relevant and whether it is still possible to implement them.
- Finally, see what tactical measures are needed to achieve the OKRs and, by extension, the strategic objectives.

When the OKRs derived from the strategy are central in the management of the company, control is maintained even in a surprising situation. Even in a case like the current pandemic, the situation is viewed by the organization through strategy and objectives, foregoing emergency and panic solutions. It can be a difficult situation, but the mechanism by which the new direction is chosen works and normalizes operations. The OKR model is not just a peacetime leadership system, it guides the whole organization in the right direction in all circumstances.

FINAL WORDS

We have equipped you with all the information we wish we had when we first started implementing the OKR model. From time to time, also we read the book to refresh our memory about the ideas we have written. Now, it's your turn — to not only take the model into practice but maybe also to teach us something new.

When we published the Finnish version in 2020, we thought that OKRs and related understanding would develop fast. Then again, we didn't understand the speed of the change. It has been tremendous. Therefore, we are still predicting that the OKR model will develop fast in the future. Many new companies and corporations publicly talk about their OKR usage.

We'd like to hear about you and your experiences when you put what you learned into practice. Please share your experiences on social media. We have been using tag #implementingokrs. We're following and responding to that one.

The world, theory and practice alike, are in constant motion. Therefore, please join us at: https://fast-track-execution.com. On the website, we have for you at least three actionable offerings.

- A webinar once every quarter.
- Directions on how to join an OKR community.
- A method how for contacting the authors.

If you notice errors or flaws in the book or want to send other feedback, you can do so using the form on the site. We are also happy to hear about your feelings and thoughts about the book and the OKR model.

An impressive OKR scene has already started to form in Finland. If you want to join the discussion and help develop the OKR model, see the instructions on the site. Many organizations and leaders are happy to share their lessons and experiences, as we learned when writing this book. They will give you a boost when starting to implement OKRs.

Ultimately, though, what matters is getting started. With this book, you have everything you need to do that. We wish you courage and continued enthusiasm on your journey!

APPENDIX 1: TEMPLATES FOR THE OKR YEAR

This appendix provides a few tools to boost the adoption of the OKR model. An assortment of different templates for OKR events, such as planning workshops and colloquialisms, have been collected into the appendix. With these templates, it is possible to prepare for events a little quicker than if you were to plan the entire event from scratch.

These templates are needed both for the implementation of the OKR model and for use with the model throughout the first OKR year.

The point is not to implement them literally. Like the OKR model, these templates should be applied to the needs and starting points of your own organization. With the help of a template, an agenda or event will be completed with significantly less effort and will be heading in the right direction.

There are five templates in the appendix and they deal with the project plan for the implementation of the OKR model, presenting the OKR model to the staff, the first OKR workshops, the quarterly planning and the handling of concerns about change.

1. Rough project plan for implementing the OKR model

The project plan is used to describe the implementation of the OKR model throughout the enterprise. Completing a project plan helps you answer the most frequently asked questions and forces you to consider the key steps of implementation before you start. We have included six of the most common aspects of the project plan in the template.

Project Objective

Before the start of the project, it is worth crystallizing the objective. Generally speaking, the objective of adopting the OKR model is **to bring strategy into everyday work and to improve business** by improving operations and the organization.

Of course, every organization needs to have a problem worth fixing, such as aligning the activities of the organization, improving the implementation of strategic objectives or enhancing the organization's ability to change. In addition, the objective should be fundamentally related to the strategy of the company. If the objective is not strategy-driven, it should be reconsidered.

Project organization, i.e., human resources

The second task is to determine who is responsible for the progress of the project and the implementation of the OKR model.

The project organization ideally includes the following:

1. Leadership team **sponsor**, who brings the management perspective into the implementation,
2. **internal champion**, who is an expert on the OKR model and is from within the organization,
3. **an employee representative**, who can bring the staff point of view.

See section 4.2 *The implementation project* for further reasons.

Schedule for the deployment project

The implementation of the OKR model requires a period of about a year in a slightly larger organization. Yes, the benefits begin as soon as the first objectives are discussed, but getting every part of the OKR model implemented takes time. Getting the entire organization to follow the OKR model should follow the schedule below.

- **First Quarter:**
  - **Leadership team** has OKRs derived from strategy.
  - The first goal of each team is to get acquainted with the OKR management system through materials or training.
- **Second Quarter:** All teams have OKRs.
- **Third Quarter:** Tracking is active and key results are predominantly numeric.
- **Fourth Quarter:** Retrospectives are used and OKRs are a part of the organization's annual clock.

Costs and procurement

Before the start of the project, you should calculate the possible costs and seek approval for them. The costs of an OKR project typically consist of using an outside consultant, the salary of the internal champion, the OKR software and, of course, acquiring quality literature explaining the OKR model for a part of the organization. If the training and workshops are held away from the office, they also generate some expenses.

Some organizations also want to calculate the amount of billable work time lost. More time will be needed in the beginning as objective setting is learned and new practices are established. Even for the smallest organization's weekly meetings, retrospectives and quarterly planning take between 1 and 2 working days per employee per quarter.

On the other hand, it is worth remembering that in reality there are no separate OKR meetings. In the long run, the OKR model integrates into the current management system. If the company already has weekly meetings and is accustomed to planning activities and reviewing past endeavors, then no additional costs will be generated after the learning period. Moreover, after a successful implementation, the OKR model can be calculated to pay for itself multiple times over in a year.

Communication

Communication is an essential part of the implementation of the OKR model and is the job of the internal champion. A communication plan is good to have so that it does not get forgotten and should be a regular part of the project and its progress. We have covered the subject comprehensively in Chapter Five; Managing expectations and leading people. You can find more tips for communication situations and how to lead expectations during deployment there.

Stakeholders

As always with projects, it is essential to keep different stakeholders informed of the situation and involved in the progress of the project. Stakeholders in the implementation of the OKR model are first and foremost internal.

The main stakeholders are the leadership team of the organization and every person in a managerial position, as well as the people in the project team. Since OKRs are strategy derivatives, one of the main stakeholders is the organization's board of directors. Its role in monitoring the strategy implementation is essential. Each stakeholder should be addressed in a manner typical to the organization, whether it's slots at management team meetings, project reports or a monthly meeting.

2. First OKR Model Demonstration Event

When the OKR model is implemented, it needs to be introduced to many stakeholders within the organization. The first demonstration is likely to be to managers who, in turn, need to spread the OKR model further to their respective teams. The following lists the main titles and substances from which the presentation event and the presentation material may be constructed.

- **Objective of implementing the OKR model**
    - The first thing to share is that the project is about bringing the strategy closer to everyday life.
    - Second, it's about improving the business — not a carbon-copy implementation of a particular theory.
    - It is often good to explain the story of what the world and everyday life looks like today and what it should look like after the OKR model is implemented. It is useful to emphasize repeatedly that the implementation is a journey.
    - It's also good to let people know how the company wants to involve employees better in planning and influencing.
- **Brief introduction of the OKR model**
    - At this point, you need to present the OKR theory, at least the objectives, key results and tasks and the quarterly cycle.
    - You might want to name other organizations using the model to build credibility in the success of the model.
    - At this point, it is worth promising that in the following workshop, the theory will be explained in more detail.
- **Executive Summary of Organization Strategy**
    - OKRs are a tool for implementing the strategy, so the next thing we need to recap is the organization strategy from which the OKRs are derived.
- **Strategic objectives of the company as OKRs**
    - At this point, it is good to have the strategic objectives of the organization described as objectives under the OKR model and ideas for key results, if possible. At the very least, it's good to have an example of a single objective and key result that can be identified as being based on the organization's strategy.
    - Promise that the managers' objectives will be managed in cooperation with them.
    - If at this stage there is already an idea of adaptations with the OKR model, they can be explained at a general level and reiterated in the workshops.

- **Benefits**
  - Listing and explaining the benefits of adopting the OKR model in the organization.
- **Organizing for the implementation of the OKR model**
  - What is relevant at this point is to state that the model has the support of the leadership team. It will be difficult at times, but the implementation of the model will not be abandoned after the first few difficulties.
  - If a consultant has been selected to support the implementation, an introduction should be made.
  - The internal champion's role is introduced and everyone is informed that the champion will be selected from among them when the time is appropriate to do so. It is recommended that the internal champion is selected before the wider model presentation or before scheduling starts. Some organizations introduce the model tentatively and ask for volunteers, which works too.
- **Dealing with the most common OKR model issues**
  - At the end of this chapter, there is a series of frequently asked questions. When you have an answer ready for them the first time around, it is easier for everyone.
  - Tell people how and where to ask specific questions when they arise. For example, chat channels, the organization's intranet, or the reception time allocated to the internal champion's calendar are good methods.
- **Implementation plan**
  - A rough schedule. You can find it at the beginning of this chapter.
- **Final words**
  - It is to provide the best possible package of materials so that people do not have to rely on search engines and get contradictory materials.
  - Finally, iterate that:
    - The aim of adopting the OKR model is to implement strategy and improve business — not the model itself.
    - The purpose is to implement it together and learn along the way.
    - Practicing using the OKR model is permitted.

3. OKR implementation workshop

It is good to allocate enough time for the first workshop. The exact amount of time depends a lot on the clarity of the organization's strategy and the depth of work, that is, required to get to know the OKR model. Some organizations need a few workdays, others can get started within two afternoons. The most important thing is to create a solid foundation to further build on.

Events can be held at the organization's own office or elsewhere, in a place that is away from the everyday bustle. The need for isolation depends on the ability of the participants to concentrate. Successful implementations have been initiated both ways.

Preparing for the event

To make the common working time-efficient, pre-reading about the basics of the OKR model is recommended. The summary of the organization's strategy is additionally valuable pre-reading material.

Day One
1. Recap reason for the implementation of the OKR model
2. OKR model theory in-depth
    a. A quiz of 10 questions about OKR theory
3. Company-specific application of the OKR model
    a. 10 questions about organization-specific applications
4. Deriving objectives from strategy
    a. Strategy needs to be divided into objectives. At this point, there could still be a lot of them.
    b. Section 3.2 *Long-term objectives are derived from the strategy* contains some suggestions for this section.
5. Recapping the day
    a. There are probably more than five objectives. They are yet a complete collection of strategy derived objectives. In addition, several key results have been considered.
6. Reflection for the evening and early morning
    a. How do we organize these objectives so that the strategy will succeed?
    b. Which ones can we leave out?
    c. Which of them need to be formulated more carefully?
7. Questions and thoughts

Additional workshop day(s)
1. Questions and thoughts
2. Recapping the reason for the implementation of the OKR model
3. OKR theory: different ways to make key results measurable
   a. See the following sections for more details:
      i. 2.3.5 Key results are not yes/no results
      ii. 2.3.6 Progress can be a key result
      iii. 2.3.7 How trust can be a key result
4. OKR theory: SMART
   a. See Section 2.3.4 The SMART key result
5. Specifying strategic objectives continues
6. Prioritizing strategic objectives
   a. Depending on the size of the organization, this can take one whole working day.
7. Defining key results
   a. Depending on the organization, this too may take one working day.
8. The outcomes of the day or days
   a. The outcome should be the objectives and key results for the first OKR quarter.
   b. Both key results and metering will most likely need to be clarified throughout the quarter.
9. Questions and thoughts

Other workshop topics

Depending on the organization, the following topics may be addressed quickly or require a full day of your workshop:
1. Integrating the OKR model into the current management system
   a. The changes may range from a few agenda changes to updating the quality management system.
2. Organizational levels in which the OKR model is implemented
   a. Initially, the leadership team will spend one quarter on the OKR model itself. After that, all the organization levels to which the model will be implemented must be decided.
   b. Are there people involved who would benefit from personal OKRs?
3. OKR Software Training
   a. A whiteboard and Excel may be good starting points, but in a slightly larger or more distributed organization, OKR software

is a must. Educating all people in the software is in itself its own transformation project.

An alternative to a series of workshops is for a consultant and an internal champion, together with the CEO, to define a draft and proposal as a basis for discussion. This greatly accelerates the start, but usually means that the model is not internalized as well in the beginning. Our preference is to use the model described in this chapter at the beginning, as it saves a lot of time in the future.

4. Preparing for the quarterly workshop

Once the OKR model is in use, careful preparation of workshops related to quarterly planning is very important. Sometimes it might start to feel like OKR workshops are progressing on their own. This is the time when it is especially important to go through all the basics, to ensure that the OKRs are aligned with the strategy and present knowledge.

Each quarter ends with a retrospective, described in Section 3.5.6 *Retrospectives*. If the organization has a chance to get the results of the retrospectives before the planning of the next quarterly objectives begins, it is worth collecting to support the planning. In this way, lessons affect future work.

The following is a list of things that are usually done in the planning workshop. The person running the workshop should go through the list lightly but thoughtfully and see what issues are important for the next workshop. If any of the issues are obvious to the workshop participants, there is no need to address them. On the other hand, if you feel like a recap is necessary, then it is necessary.

1. OKR and Strategy alignment
   a. A look at strategy materials
   b. Update to strategic objectives
   c. A recap of annual strategic objectives
   d. A recap of strategic choices. What to do? What not to do?
2. How has the OKR management system worked as a system?
   a. What data has been obtained from retrospectives in terms of systemic operation?
   b. How systematic has our organization been? Have objectives and key results been updated weekly?

c. Have all teams and individuals been able to update their objectives?
   d. Have objectives and key results guided operations?
   e. If they haven't, what changes are needed to make it so?
   f. When you bring up developing the management system in a workshop, limit the suggestions for improvement that people can offer to just three. If you don't do this, this may eat up a lot of time.
   g. ⇒ Improvement ideas for the management system.
3. Changes during the quarter
   a. Changes in the operating environment
      i. Did covid or some other similar surprising thing appear during the quarter?
      ii. Are there any changes in the operating environment that need to be taken into account?
         1. competitors?
         2. customers?
         3. products?
         4. employees?
         5. technology?
         6. organization?
         7. work environment and equipment/machinery?
         8. infrastructure?
   b. Recorded ideas for change
      i. What thoughts and ideas regarding changes did we record during the previous quarter? Will they affect the planning of the upcoming quarter?
      ii. Does the strategy need to be challenged based on these ideas?
   c. Higher-level changes in the organization
      i. If there have been any changes in the organization's top-level objectives, they must be taken into account.
4. Reflection on the previous quarter and a look at the next quarter
   a. Demonstrating progress.
      i. How did we progress? Point this out through a few key results.
   b. Objective
      i. Why was this objective set for the previous quarter?
      ii. What kind of key results did we get?
      iii. Is the objective done? Will it be replaced or reformulated for the next quarter?

      iv. Key Results
   1. How has the key result been achieved during the quarter?
   2. Will the key results continue to be tracked in the next quarter? Or will it be replaced by another key result?
   3. Repeat the same steps for each key result of the objective.
   c. Repeat Objective Steps a and b for all quarterly objectives
5. The end result will be the agenda for the workshop

5. Concerns about change — 10 questions and answers

1. Q: Will OKRs replace the strategy?
A: They won't. OKRs are derived from organizational strategy, allowing OKRs to help implement the desired change from it. The strategy is implemented into everyday life by using the OKR model.

See Section 1.1 *How OKRs align the whole organization* for more details.

2. Q: What is the difference between OKRs and KPI metrics?
A: OKRs are outcome centric objectives and key results that help execute strategy. OKRs and key results can each have a maximum of five aims and/or actions. The KPI metrics indicate the organization's situation at any given time. There may be dozens of them in an organization.

See Section 2.6.2 *Objectives are set at the team level*

3. Q: How are OKRs factored into performance reviews?
A: It is not possible to judge people's performance directly based on the numeric values of the OKRs because there may be different amounts of stretch in the key results. The OKRs are brought up by the manager in performance reviews, but the discussion is primarily about the manager's interpretation of performance.

See section 7.5 *OKRs will impact your performance reviews*, for more detail.

4. Q: What if other people see that I failed?
A: Everyone is going to fail. If all objectives have been achieved after a quarter, there has been insufficient stretch in the objectives. The goal of the OKR

model is not to track the success or failure of individuals, but to focus on learning and achieving objectives together.

See section 5.6 *Radical transparency is the default.*

5. Q: Will my financial rewards change?

A: Financial rewards are not tied to OKR targets because stretch targets don't work with them. OKRs do, however, bring strategy to everyday life. If the strategic objectives are realized, the financial rewards tied to them will remain.

See section 7.4 *Rewards and OKRs*, for more detail.

6. Q: How often do I need to update OKRs?

A: Every week. Sometimes there may be situations where every other week there is a better cadence, but usually, OKRs are updated weekly. This helps keep the objective in the crosshair and reflect on how confident you are about reaching your objective (i.e., what is the confidence value of the objective).

See section 3.5.1 *Tracking cadence in OKRs.*

7. Q: I don't have time to plan these objectives. There's already too much to do!

A: Yes. Often there's a lot to do. On the other hand, the purpose of implementing the OKR model is to create peace for the quarter, so that we can focus on doing what is right for the strategy. Because there's a lot to do, something needs to be left out. Making these choices creates a calm working environment.

See section 3.1.5 *Peace and concentration during the quarterly OKRs.*

8. Q: What is the difference between the key result and the task?

A: The key result is a number from which one can see the progress has been made on the associated objective. Each key result can involve many tasks.

See sections 2.3 *Key results* and 2.4 *Tasks*, for more detail.

9. Q: Will OKRs replace development projects?

A: No. OKRs are objectives and key results — not projects. It's up to the OKRs to demonstrate what's important right now. The organization continues to utilize development projects and their progress will be tracked through OKRs.

See section 2.3.6 *Progress can be a key result.*

10. Q: All objectives and new ideas are important; no project can wait three months. How do I choose only five objectives?

A: Things will actually be completed more quickly by working on a smaller number of objectives at the same time. While it may feel like something will be left on hold, eventually, all projects will be completed faster when done sequentially rather than simultaneously. OKRs mean there is permission from the leadership team to prioritize work, and the best project is a completed project.

See section 2.2.2. *Only up to five objectives at a time*

APPENDIX 2: ARCHIVE OF CASE-STUDIES

Ambientia

Ambientia is an IT company that has for over 20 years combined human understanding, business and technology. Ambientia's mission is to build lasting and tangible ability for its customers to succeed in the future. Founded in 1996 in Hämeenlinna, the company employs nearly 200 employees, has seven offices and operates in two countries. The book's co-author, Henri Sora, is Ambientia's former COO and board member. He began implementing OKRs in Ambientia in 2018.

https://ambientia.fi/

Interviewed:
Jussi Haaja, OKR Champion

Case Stories:

Aiming to improve the maturity of operations by using an information security index as a key result *(section 2.3.4)*
Ambientia invests in aligning its objectives *(section 3.3.2)*
Ambientia's internal champion served as OKR Champion *(section 4.2.2)*
Repurposing Jira — for example, Ambientia *(section 4.3.3)*

Aucor

Aucor Ltd. is a high-quality WordPress office founded in 2007. Aucor was sold in 2019 to Markkinointiakatemia MAK Oy (Ltd).

https://www.aucor.fi/

Interviewed:
Janne Jääskeläinen, former CEO

Case story:

Reflection and engagement with KOAN – case study Aucor *(section 4.3.5)*

Futurice

Futurice is a nearly 20-year-old IT consultancy house operating in several countries, with eight offices and employs over 600 employees. Futurice has delivered more than 3,000 projects and the consortium also includes Aito.ai, Columbia Road and Tentimes. Futurice's OKR deployment launched in January 2019.

https://futurice.com/

Interviewed:
Viljami Väisänen, Manager, Strategic Development & Deployment

Case Stories:

OKRs can also be graded "prematurely" *(in section 2.3.8)*
Futurice's internal champion created his own OKR materials *(in section 4.2.2)*
The OKR journey – Futurice case study *(section 4.2.3)*
Futurice's tips for the CEO or internal champion *(in section 4.5)*

Google

Google LLC is an American company founded in 1998 that has created many of the staples of Internet services, including Google, Gmail, and the web browser Google Chrome. The OKR model has become known specifically through Google, where the model was implemented as early as the 1990s. Google has said it has reached its targets tenfold using the OKR model.

Interviewed:

Hanna Kivelä, Sector Lead, Netherlands

Case Stories:

The OKR model is important to Google for the speed of change *(section 1.5)*
Google reWork guidelines *(section 3.3.1)*
Google's OKR tools are very simple *(in section 4.3)*

HappyOrNot

HappyOrNot from Tampere specializes in measuring customer experience. The company is known for its feedback device that allows you to evaluate your experience using four different emoticons. In addition to the physical device, HappyOrNot also measures the quality of the customer or employee experience online and helps its customers improve the customer experience based on the data collected. The OKR and CFR models have been used byHappyOrNot since early 2019.

https://www.happy-or-not.com/fi/

Interviewed:

Eve Lennon, Director, Product Development
Heidi Hyysalo, People & Talent Manager, OKR internal champion
Sami Hero, COO

Case story:

HappyOrNot ditches performance reviews for CFR model *(section 7.5)*

Heltti

Heltti is the fastest growing health services company in Europe, implementing welfare and health services, especially for knowledge workers. Heltti operates in seven locations and employs more than 60 staff members. Heltti is backed by professional investors such as Risto Siilasmaa's First Fellow and English Tearoom of Paulig. The OKR model was implemented at Heltti in early 2019.

https://heltti.fi/

Interviewed:
Timo Lappi, CEO

Case story:

Values are memorized, OKRs not *(section 7.3)*

Labrox

Labrox is a Turku-based technology company that plans and manufactures plate readers. They are laboratory instruments used to study the reactions in various fluid samples. Plater readers are widely used in research, drug development and quality assurance, and diagnostics. Labrox had a revenue of 3.9 million euros in 2019 and the company currently employs 20 people. Author Henri Sora is the managing director of Labrox.

https://www.labrox.fi/

Case story:
OKRs on a whiteboard – case study Labrox *(section 4.3.2)*

Motiva

Motiva is the Finnish national sustainability company. Motiva provides public and private sector operators and consumers with information and services that enable them to make resource-efficient, impactful, and sustainable choices. The OKR model has been a part of their annual clock since early 2020.

https://www.motiva.fi/

Interviewed:

Vesa Silfver, CEO

Case story:

Motiva's strategic annual clock is built in Plandisc *(section 7.2)*

Nixu

Nixu is a cybersecurity company of 400 professionals, operating in the international market. The company aims to keep digital society functioning and help businesses make the most of digitalization safely. Nixu began to use the OKR model on a more permanent basis in 2020, after a one-year pilot period.

https://www.nixu.com/

Interviewed:

Jonatan Henriksson, Head of Digital Business

Case story:

Cybersecurity company Nixu uses tertiles instead of quarters *(in section3.1.4)*
Nixu rewards based on financial figures *(section 7.4)*

Talented

Talented Ltd, specializing in recruitment and growth consultancy in the IT industry, is a fast-growing startup. In three years, Talented has developed into a three-business organization, employing nearly thirty staff in three locations. Talented adopted the OKR model at the end of 2019.

https://talented.fi/

Interviewed:

Teemu Tiilikainen, COO

Case story:

Talented provides themes, teams decide objectives *(in section 3.3.2)*

Tangible Growth

Tangible Growth, less formally known as TG, is a startup specializing in transformation management and strategy implementation. TG's methodology and SaaS tool have helped companies implement strategy in everyday life and accelerate transformations. Tangible Growth's solutions allow you to foster organizational ability to change and to respond to uncertainty. OKRs are an integral part of both TG's methodology and software. The co-author of the book, Juuso Hämäläinen, is the founder and CEO of Tangible Growth.

https://www.tangible-growth.com/

Case story:

TG software focuses on the strategy – case study Tangible Growth *(section 4.3.4)*

The Weekdone

Weekdone is an OKR software vendor whose software is ideal for companies, departments, or teams looking to improve productivity and work toward common objectives. The software allows each employee to see through OKRs and weekly plans what is being worked on. Weekdone is an Estonian startup founded in 2009.

https://weekdone.com/

Interviewed:
Mirell Põllumäe, Customer Success Manager
Richard Snaith, Customer Success Manager

Case story:

Weekdone has a built-in TV dashboard *(section 7.3)*

Other case stories:

OKRs for the entrepreneur *(in section 2.2.6)*
-Elisa Heikura, EHOY

"If you understand how the system works, let us know" *(section 2.5)*
- Anonymous

Planning objectives directly from the company's objectives *(section 3.4.2)*
- Anonymous

Incorrect use of the OKR model increases the amount of chaos *(in section 6.5)*
- Anonymous

"How Might We" or HMW is Timo Herttua's favorite *(in section 3.2.2)*
-Timo Herttua, Hoxhunt

What does management commitment look like? *(in section 4.1.3)*
- Antti Kirjavainen, Flowa

From performance reviews to development planning — the Reactor model *(section 7.5)*
- Reaktor

SOURCES

BOOKS

Acuff, J. (2017). *Finish: Give Yourself the Gift of Done.* Portfolio.

Allen, D. (2001). *Getting Things Done: The Art of Stress-Free Productivity.* Penguin Books.

Brown, B. (2018). *Dare to Lead: Brave Work. Tough Conversations. Whole Hearts.* Random House. (Suomennettu: Rohkaiseva johtaja)

Buckingham, M. & Goodall, A. (2019). *Nine Lies About Work: A Freethinking Leader's Guide to the Real World.* Harvard Business Review Press.

Collins, J. (2004). *Built to Last: Successful Habits of Visionary Companies (Good to Great).* Harper Business.

Doerr, J. (2018). *Measure What Matters: How Google, Bono, and the Gates Foundation Rock the World with OKRs.* Portfolio.

Goldratt, E. (2014). *The Goal: A Process of Ongoing Improvement, 30th Anniversary Edition edition.* North River Press. (Suomennettu: Tavoite)

Grove, A. (1983). *High Output Management.* Random House.

Heen, S. & Stone, D. (2014). *Thanks for the Feedback: The Science and Art of Receiving Feedback Well.* Viking.

Henriksson, J. (2018). *Building a Strategy Implementation Framework for a Consultancy Company.* (YAMK-opinnäytetyö Metropolia) Saatavuus: https://www.theseus.fi/handle/10024/157260

Horowitz, B. (2019). *What You Do Is Who You Are: How to Create Your Business Culture.* Harper Business.

Kim, G., Behr, K. & Spafford, G. (2013). *The Phoenix Project: A Novel about IT, DevOps, and Helping Your Business Win.* IT Revolution Press

Lencioni, P. (2002). *The Five Dysfunctions of a Team: A Leadership Fable.* Jossey-Bass. (Suomennettu: Viisi toimintahäiriötä tiimissä)

Lencioni, P. (2007). *The Three Signs of a Miserable Job: A Fable for Managers (And Their Employees)*. Jossey-Bass.

Newport, C. (2016). *Deep Work: Rules for Focused Success in a Distracted World*. YCS Publishers

Niven, P. R. & Lamorte B. (2016). *Objectives and Key Results: Driving Focus, Alignment, and Engagement with OKRs.* Wiley.

Pink, D. (2009). *Drive: The Surprising Truth About What Motivates Us*. Riverhead Books.

Sinek, S. (2011). *Start with Why: How Great Leaders Inspire Everyone to Take Action*. Portfolio.

Sinek, S. (2014). *Leaders Eat Last: Why Some Teams Pull Together and Others Don't*. Portfolio.

Sinek, S. (2019). *The Infinite Game*. Portfolio.

Tague, N. (2005). The quality toolbox (2nd ed.). ASQ Quality Press.

Tamm, J. W. & Luyetin, R. J. (2004). *Radical Collaboration: Five Essential Skills to Overcome Defensiveness and Build Successful Relationships.* Harper Business.

Torkkola, S. (2015). *Lean asiantuntijatyön johtamisessa*. Alma Talent.

Tracy, B. (2017). *Eat That Frog!:* 21 Great Ways to Stop Procrastinating and Get More Done in Less Time. Berrett-Koehler Publishers.

Wodtke, C. (2016). *Introduction to OKRs*. O'Reilly Media.

Wodtke, C. (2016). *Radical Focus: Achieving Your Most Important Goals with Objectives and Key Results.* Cucina Media LLC.

ONLINE SOURCES

Castro, F. (2020). *Stretch Goals: How Ambitious should Your OKRs be*. https://felipecastro.com/en/okr/understanding-stretch-goals/ (Referenced 9.5.2020)

Google (2018). *Guide: Set goals with OKRs*.https://rework.withgoogle.com/guides/set-goals-with-okrs/ (Referenced 3.4.2020)

GTMHub (2020). *All about OKRs and why They Matter*. https://gtmhub.com/okrs (Referenced 4.4.2020)

Horowitz, B. (2011). *Peacetime CEO/Wartime CEO.* https://a16z.com/2011/04/14/peacetime-ceowartime-ceo-2 (Referenced 20.5.2020)

Huy, Q. (2016). *Five Reasons Most Companies Fail at Strategy Execution.* https://knowledge.insead.edu/blog/insead-blog/five-reasons-most-companies-fail-at-strategy-execution-4441 (Referenced 12.5.2020)

IDEO.org (2020). *Design Kit: How Might We.* https://www.designkit.org/methods/3 (Referenced 16.4.2020)

Lippitt, M. (1987) & Knoster T. (1991). *Leading and Managing Complex Change.* https://sergiocaredda.eu/organisation/tools/models-the-lippit-knoster-model-for-managing-complex-change/. (Referenced 20.5.2020)

Spotify (2014). *Spotify engineering culture (part 1).* https://labs.spotify.com/2014/03/27/spotify-engineering-culture-part-1/ (Referenced 3.4.2020)

Tingvall, Johanna Bolin. (2016). *Life after OKRs – balancing between chaos and structure* | HR Blog. https://hrblog.spotify.com/2016/09/27/keeping-your-balance-between-chaos-and-structure/ (Referenced 8.4.2020)

Tingvall, Johanna Bolin. (2016). *Why individual OKRs don't work for us* | HR Blog. https://hrblog.spotify.com/2016/08/15/our-beliefs/ (Referenced 8.4.2020)

Other

Nixu Oyj. (2019). *OKR Strategy Tool Documentation*

WRITERS

Juuso Hämäläinen

Juuso wants to improve the management culture and performance of organizations globally. He is used to managing business and change and is an executive coach. He is the founder and CEO of the startup Tangible Growth, where he and his team have produced a modern change management model and built a software service around it. The change management model and the tool help leaders foster enterprise agility and drive a high-performance culture.

Juuso has served as an advisor for several organizations and sparred with boards and management teams, especially regarding strategy implementation and extensive cultural changes. He has also been a speaker and guest lecturer in several eMBA courses.

Henri Sora

Henri is an experienced change and business manager who has worked in the ICT environment for over 20 years. Initially working as a programmer, Henri has grown through the roles of Chief Technology Officer and Chief Operating Officer to become a CEO and board member. Henri has experience in managing technology and software organizations. He currently serves as the CEO of Labrox.

Henri is interested in the continuous development of businesses, people, and himself. Curiosity has driven him to graduate from an eMBA, as well as to spar with and help grow new directors to the boards of several organizations. He is active in organizations particularly regarding business development and increasing operational maturity and has introduced the OKR model to several experienced leaders.